# FAILED CHILD WELFARE POLICY

*Family Preservation and
the Orphaning of Child Welfare*

**Janet R. Hutchinson**
with Cecelia E. Sudia

University Press of America,® Inc.
Lanham · New York · Oxford

Copyright © 2002 by
University Press of America,® Inc.
4720 Boston Way
Lanham, Maryland 20706
UPA Acquisitions Department (301) 459-3366

12 Hid's Copse Rd.
Cumnor Hill, Oxford OX2 9JJ

**Library of Congress Cataloging-in-Publication Data**

Hutchinson, Janet R.
Failed child welfare policy : family preservation and the orphaning
of child welfare / Janet R. Hutchinson with Cecelia E. Sudia.
p.   cm
Includes bibliographical references and index.
1. Child welfare—United States. 2. Foster children—United States.
3. Social work with children—United States. 4. Family social
work—United States. I. Sudia, Cecelia E. II. Title.

HV741 .H85 2002
362.7'0973—dc21         2002018724 CIP

ISBN 0-7618-2249-6 (pbk. : alk. paper)

*This book is dedicated to*
*Jennifer, Jim, Steve, Elizabeth, and Ted.*

# Contents

# Preface

This book is a study of several discourses that intersect in the area of public child welfare. It is based, in part, on our personal and professional experiences during a period when we were both involved with family preservation grants sponsored by the Department of Health and Human Services' Children's Bureau—one as project director of the University of Iowa's National Resource Center on Family Based Services[1], and the other as the federal project officer who oversaw the administration of family preservation and other discretionary grants related to child welfare.

Cecelia Sudia, who contributed the historical content related to the Children's Bureau in Chapter 4, and background information on prevention programs described in Chapter 2, did her graduate work in the sociology of the family and worked for many years in the Children's Bureau until her recent retirement in 1999. She now lives in Pittsburgh, Pennsylvania, with her husband, Ted. Cecelia's extensive archive of materials dating back to her early years with the bureau was used in researching this work.

Janet Hutchinson holds degrees in sociology, public administration, and public policy; she is also an adoptive parent, has worked in child welfare –principally in national resource centers, and as deputy director of a mid-sized urban public child welfare agency. She is currently an associate professor of public administration. Both have worked in a consulting capacity with public and private child welfare agencies—on contract or by grant in Janet's case, and as a federal children's bureau resource person and project officer, in Cecelia's. In these capacities, we have seen programs come and go over the years, have worked with agencies in every state and can attest to their similarities, their strengths and their weaknesses. It is principally these positions, and our combined sixty years' experience, that provide the background for this book.

Although no longer directly involved in the family-based services movement, we remain convinced that the limited resources that policy makers extend to children and families could be put to better use by seeking and addressing "root causes" of family dysfunction, and by giving families a chance to succeed rather than standing by until they fail. We think most people would agree with us with the proviso that children are not left in dangerous circumstances. We would beg the question with the rejoinder, "What constitutes a dangerous circumstance and could such circumstances be altered with removal of the sources of danger rather than the child?"

Maintaining the integrity of families remains a goal worth pursuing. However, until we can understand the reasons that family-centered services are foundering, it is unlikely, in our view, that these programs will replace the current system of child welfare services in the United States. It is our purpose in writing this book to begin a process of reflection and analysis that will lead to a reconstruction of child welfare services as family-centered while welcoming and engaging multiple discourses.

We would like to acknowledge the many people we worked with over the years, too many to name—we learned something from each one. Child welfare workers are heroes in our view; it is the system in which they work that is lacking. We would also like to acknowledge our families and the friends who supported us in this endeavor, and offer a special thank you to David Farmer and Jeanne Giovannoni for reading and commenting on drafts.

---

[1] The resource center is still active at the University of Iowa. It was renamed the National Resource Center for Family Centered Practice several years ago.

# Introduction

Newspaper reporter, David Nicholson (2000), describes the feelings of futility and anger that he experienced while seeking help for his godchild, a fourteen year old boy whose foster mother could no longer cope with his aggressive behavior. In the time that it took Nicholson to secure the psychological evaluation and educational testing required for placement in the residential center where the boy could receive the treatment he needed, the bed space was gone. Furthermore, his godchild experienced three different placements in the interim nine weeks' time. This is not an isolated occurrence, particularly for young African-American males. Nicholson thought he could do what the boy's former foster mother could not—thinking that she hadn't tried hard enough. He presumed that with his reporter's know how, he could locate sources and navigate bureaucracies but he was wrong.

Most of us have felt similar frustration when seeking help from local service providers—tedious telephone menus, inconvenient hours of operation (they work the same hours we work), and unresponsive workers give one an appreciation for Nicholson's frustration. Of course, the difference in magnitude of importance between a city worker rectifying a missed trash pick-up, and a caseworker finding a child an acceptable home should be significant. But in most of our communities, it apparently is not.

The state's children are precious to us only in the abstract. In reality, they appear to be disposable. In the nation's service communities, multiple voices (discourses) assert their claims on parts of a family's life—health and mental health, school, work, housing, among others. These voices could be exploited on behalf of troubled families and children; instead, the absence of effective leadership in the fields most closely connected with the work of child welfare—social work, public administration and mental health—has left it orphaned.

This book is about the public child welfare system in the United States viewed through the lens of the largely failed family preservation movement—a postmortem that presents an opportunity to examine some of the larger system's more obvious weaknesses. The philosophy behind the services driving the family preservation movement did, and may still hold an opportunity to alter substantively the way public child welfare is managed and services are offered to families and children. However, a transformation to family-centered services is unlikely to occur until the public acknowledges that the child welfare system in the United States is dangerously troubled and that an engaged citizenry and collective action is needed to reform it.

Neither is substantive action likely to occur until the social work discipline reclaims the child welfare system it has orphaned and practicing child welfare professionals and administrators refrain from hiding behind the veil of confidentiality[1] that has been used to keep critics at bay. Inviting public scrutiny and help from other disciplines and the communities that child welfare agencies serve, may be a difficult pill to swallow; nevertheless, without outside help, it is our view that the child welfare field is doomed to repeat its failures.

Bearing on these prescriptive demands is a clash of discourses that prevents shared problem solving. When professionals prize disciplinary boundaries over interdisciplinary pragmatism, opportunities are lost. Multidisciplinary support for coherent and compassionate child welfare policies is all the more important since the principal advocates for other child-focused public policy interests are absent in child welfare: children's parents. Parents are the chief advocates for their children's education, their health and mental health, and for special needs, for example, services to the developmentally disabled. Advocacy for the health and well-being of troubled children who are poor is challenging—advocating for the health and well-being of families in which child maltreatment is present is even more so. The story of the family preservation movement provides a case in point.

The child welfare system is designed to remove children from their 'dysfunctional' families. It accomplishes this task very efficiently, the unfortunate effects on children notwithstanding. The fundamental issues that render the system of child welfare services ineffective for so many children and their families are also the issues that make it difficult for prevention programs to succeed. High caseloads, a paucity of the right kinds of community resources and under-funding, among others, are reasons enough for failure; however, there are also the artificial boundaries erected by disciplines, academics and service providers that militate against creative solutions. We approach this dilemma using discourse analysis to examine the different perspectives of principle actors in the child welfare drama and to understand the intersections of language, disciplines, and ideologies. Multiple discourses occur in the broader child welfare context; however, our interest is in the discourses that contribute to the ideological under-pinnings of U.S. child welfare policy.

These discourses are embedded in the fields of social work, public administration and family therapy, a relative newcomer to the mental health field. We purposely omit the justice system, specifically, the family court. Although federal child welfare legislation made the family court judge[2] a permanent part of foster care review in the child welfare system, a circumstance we describe in a later chapter, the three discourses that we discuss pre-date that mandate. The integration of family court into the child welfare process is a more recent result of the system's perceived incompetence and, typical of partial remedies, has become part of the problem instead of its solution.

Family preservation services are characterized as short-term, labor intensive and therapy-oriented, focusing on the family as a whole rather than exclusively on the child. This focus on the family rather than the individual child supports the view that any changes promoting stability and reasonably healthy functioning must be born by those who are central to the child's development, commonly family members. Family preservation services are a departure from the historical but still common practice of "child saving" in which children are "saved" from bad parents and placed with "good" parents. As it was originally conceived, family preservation services gave mom, dad, and kids (or whomever comprises a given family) the tools they need to figure out what their most pressing problems are, how to remedy those that they can, live less destructively with those they can not remedy, and redirect their anger away from their children.

An early family preservation initiative in St. Paul, Minnesota, known as the St. Paul Project, lasted twenty years until dissension over turf-issues among agency administrators ended it. Turf issues have also played a central role in undermining the current family preservation movement as has the ubiquitous absence of consistent local and state funding. There is little interest in spending public money on labor-intensive family preservation services, particularly when placing a child in foster care supports the illusion that something really positive is being accomplished by doing so. Nonetheless, the case can be made for funding family preservation services, and was done, briefly, during the period when the Edna McConnell Clark Foundation marketing strategy was underway.

When foundation support was later withdrawn, many local agencies lost the will to expend limited local and state political capital on a program whose own advocates were strongly split over what might charitably be described as 'best practices'. Before proceeding, a disclaimer is in order: family preservation services should not be equated or confused with efforts to politicize the idea of family by pitting so-called traditional definitions and family values against those that do not enjoy mainstream support. Such notions are well beyond the pragmatic desire of child welfare workers to work with a caring parent. The term 'family preservation' was conceived in apparent innocence of its political implications and its vague smell of formaldehyde.

Three decades of attempts to implement the family preservation approach in agencies across the country have helped us to see the weaknesses in the child welfare system that programs with fewer structural requirements and less audacious claims for success might not reveal. Some attribute the failure of family preservation to overblown claims for preventing foster care; others have suggested that artificial time limits on treatment are causal. These are indeed problems, but both are remediable. More significant are the weaknesses that originate in the child welfare system itself. Federal and state policy makers, guided by policy analysts and program developers have for some time nurtured a tendency to categorize programs according to type and function with little consideration for the effects that such divisions have on service recipients.

Clashing ideologies also impede the adoption of family preservation services, as does our tendency to approach large, unwieldy policy problems by segmenting, subdividing, and categorizing. This very human tendency to simplify complex issues can have serious consequences for families. When a family is assigned to a service unit that is designed to treat a specific problem—for example, an infant stimulation and parenting program—the family (or child) is viewed through the narrow lens of a provider who sees only one element among a constellation of family problems. Other family problems are given short shrift or ignored altogether. A mother who is distraught over her husband's abuse and unemployment has little chance of successfully using infant stimulation techniques if no effort is made to support her through the process of solving her other, equally pressing problems.

We argue that child welfare policies that do not recognize the inter-relatedness of family members and their problems have a distorting effect on the public child welfare system. Casting family preservation as just one of many categorical programs—child abuse, child neglect, foster care and adoption—subverts its original holistic approach and its potential to harmonize the cacophony of voices and ideologies, also known as discourses, that are influential in shaping the child welfare system. Service providers' tendency to categorize client's problems according to services and divisions of labor is convenient for administrators but can have grave consequences for clients.

Family preservation services are defined in Chapter 1. The point of this chapter is two-fold: to briefly describe the child welfare system, the nature of the decisions that are routinely made and the difficult circumstances under which they are made. The second point is to suggest that changes in the system will be largely cosmetic until everyone with a stake in the child welfare system accepts responsibility for it. Recognizing that family preservation sails under several different flags, the discussion centers on two models that have for some time existed side by side: one is based on the behaviorists' theories of social learning and the other, on cybernetics-systems approaches to family therapy. Also described is a 'generic' public child welfare organization: how it is structured organizationally, and what its functions are, its employees and some of the difficulties they encounter in a system that is under-funded and over-run with cases. A composite of a child neglect case is presented to illustrate the most common type of case encountered in child welfare, mundane but as important as the sensational cases we are accustomed to seeing in the newspaper.

Foster care is generally considered to be a less than optimal experience for children. The clinical view is that children do best with their biological parents unless their parents' abusive or neglectful behavior is too dangerous and unlikely to change within a period that is reasonable with respect to the child's sense of time. Chapter 2 elaborates on the foster care system that inspired the early family preservation practice models. We also discuss in this chapter, several federal initiatives that were designed to prevent foster care, including the adoption of children with special needs, a case management model called permanency planning, and the early in-home family-based services programs that were the forerunners of the family preservation programs operating today.

These initiatives were designed to reduce the growing number of children being placed in foster care (this term includes family, group home, and institutional care) or, as in the case of permanency planning, to reduce the length of time that foster children remain away from their biological families. Also described in Chapter 2, is one of the earliest family centered programs, the St. Paul Family Centered Project, which functioned for twenty years until its quarreling administrators abandoned it. Although not a therapy model (family therapy as we describe it was in its earliest stages of development during this period) the St. Paul project exemplifies many of the currently fashionable community partnership models, and is an interesting demonstration of early "family-centeredness".

The ideological differences and areas shared in common among the social work, family therapy, and public administration disciplines are explored in Chapter 3, drawing attention to the tendencies of professionals and policy makers to operationalize doable elements of a problem without taking responsibility for the consequences of the larger problem. Common in policy-making, operationalizing problems selectively has resulted in unfortunate consequences for children and families in the child welfare system, especially when the system's bureaucratic structure is designed for routine tasks, instead of the emotionally charged problems of very troubled families. The notions of 'boxism', and its suggested antidote, seriality, are introduced as a means for re-conceptualizing the organizational structure that militates against family preservation services. Boxism (Farmer, 1995) is a metaphor for the rigid structures, both conceptually and in practice, that divide people ideologically and structurally, from one another. The permeability of the walls that separate individuals, groups and disciplines, is made evident in our discussion of seriality, a concept adapted by feminist philosopher Iris Marion Young from the work of philosopher and existential humanist, Jean-Paul Sartre. It is proposed that by overcoming propensities to think and act 'in boxes' policy makers and practitioners are freed to think creatively when faced with what appear to be intractable problems. Several examples are proposed for structural changes that would make it possible to adopt a family centered philosophy in the public agency.

Family preservation services would not likely have found wide acceptance without having first been sanctioned by the Children's Bureau of the U.S. Department of Health and Human Services. Nevertheless, during the period in which the nascent family centered programs were finding supporters in the child welfare community, the

Children's Bureau was undergoing multiple reorganizations that effectively and systematically weakened its influence with child welfare agencies and national child advocacy organizations.

In Chapter 4, the federal response to family preservation services is discussed. A brief historical profile of the Children's Bureau describes the difficult period that the women of the bureau experienced during the 1960s when the welfare of poor, disorganized, and troubled families was, remarkably, the administration's concern. This is contrasted with the late1970s and 1980s when the tables turned and welfare and those who needed it were disdained and further marginalized. A neglected Children's Bureau left a vacuum in the child welfare community that was filled by private philanthropic organizations that enjoy autonomy free from external citizen involvement or public scrutiny. The new role played by these organizations was part of a Faustian bargain struck by policy makers in which the tax dollars used for child welfare programs were supplemented with foundation dollars.

Discourses that are present in the work of advocates who have been instrumental in promoting family preservation services are the subject of Chapter 5. One could argue that family preservation services and child welfare were both born out of advocacy efforts. In this chapter, a typology is developed that allows us to construe broadly the role and influence of advocates in the child welfare community. Comparisons between family preservation services and mental health services are drawn noting the similarities and differences in their efforts to gain important community support. Advocacy, we contend, is two-edged. The work of advocates is responsible for many of the more progressive changes made in child welfare over the years, not to mention the advent of child welfare itself. However, advocacy unchecked may also be divisive and destructive as the examples in Chapter 5 suggest.

Child welfare advocates have sponsored research in the hope that the findings will support their claims for a favored policy, a strategy that has backfired more than once in the short history of family preservation. Studies, with both public and private sponsorship, have been grudgingly supported and minimally financed, often requiring adherence to unrealistic time frames from beginning to end. Yet, research findings, even in studies that are clearly flawed, are used authoritatively by policy makers. Child welfare researchers must grapple with difficult methodological issues when conducting their studies, particularly in the less well-conceptualized family centered service areas. These issues include difficulties in assessing levels of client risk, operationalizing therapeutic concepts, and defining successful outcomes. However, issues of method are but one of the problems with empirical studies in child welfare and family-centered services. As others have amply noted—an absence of a serious commitment to research by potential sponsors, and the appetite for immediate, confirming answers are also contributing factors. When findings are thought to be an impediment rather than an aide to the process of policy-making, political appointees and foundation officials have been known to suppress negative or unpopular research results.

These and other issues related to research and evaluation studies are discussed in Chapter 6. Also discussed in this chapter are the family preservation evaluation studies alluded to above and several other studies that attempt to give us a picture of the broader child welfare system. Although much has already been written about the evaluations of family preservation services, we suggest that criticisms have over-emphasized positivist prescriptions, with too little emphasis on the more helpful multimethod and qualitative research designs. We suggest that positivist remedies are simply another example of boxism.

The last chapter asks the reader to imagine a re-constructed child welfare system in which multiple discourses are not only recognized but are solicited. Once again the three discourses, social work, public administration, and family therapy are examined from a re-constructing, "imagining" perspective. It is argued in this chapter that the child saving discourse that has become the mantra of child abuse prevention advocates must be open to critical interrogation. Marginalizing any voice has the effect of marginalizing all voices in a field which itself operates in the shadows of social welfare discourse. The point is made that the possibilities when thinking beyond the box—that is, the walls and categories we construct and that have been constructed in the child welfare system—are limited only by our imaginations and that the solution to this problem may lay beyond the field of social work.

As is so often the case within disciplines, dialogue is inwardly focused and the social work discipline is no exception. The plea made in this chapter is that social work's introspective gaze must be reversed to reclaim the abandoned area of child welfare, and that in this examination the barriers that prevent interdisciplinary work should be lifted. At the same time, public administration and policy, academic areas only recently open to women and minorities, are encouraged to include the social welfare of children and families among their areas of study and practice.

Family therapy, often a lonely, and isolating activity, has the keys that open a lock-box of techniques for achieving success with troubled families. However, the natural introspectiveness of therapists and their exclusionary language tends to go against open discourse. Virginia Satir and Salvador Minuchin are exceptional examples of therapist-activists—therapists willing to share their talents and techniques with public agency workers and families. These remarkable therapists amply demonstrated that skilled therapeutic interventions can alter toxic intra-familial relations, even among families known to the child welfare agency as chronically dysfunctional.

Omitted from our discussion of the child welfare system and family preservation is an examination of poverty and its relationship to child welfare issues in the United States. Neither do we discuss the systematic oppression of women and minorities in employment, inferior health care, mental health services, and education for poor and minority families, all factors to consider in reforming public child welfare services. Public and political reaction to these issues have contributed to marginalizing child welfare services and must not be overlooked in re-constructing family and children's services in this country.

In telling the family preservation practice story, we bring a perspective built on our own experiences and understanding of the events that occurred over a 20 year period. Many of the principals that were involved in the family preservation movement during that time have gone on to different projects, some have died, others are still practicing in the field. Although we may not have agreed with the positions that each espoused, there is little doubt in our minds that those with whom we were professionally engaged were dedicated to improving the welfare of children and their families.

---

## Notes

[1] There are good reasons to protect client information. We refer to the practice of using confidentiality to insulate the agency, not to protect the client.

[2] The names used for the court vary among the jurisdictions. We use the term family court, since it is descriptive.

# Chapter 1

---

## The Failed Public Child Welfare System

### *Introduction*

Ahsianea Carzan, aged five, died in a crowded, roach-infested apartment with bare cupboards and three siblings in New York City's Bronx Borough (Bernstein 1998). Ahsianea's twenty-four year old mother, a victim of domestic violence and orphaned herself, has been the subject of numerous complaints to the city's Administration for Children's Service. Like so many of the agency's cases, this one is complicated by the child's severe cerebral palsy, a bitter custody dispute between her divorced parents, and stunning poverty.

Her case had been referred to a private agency for services, and although it was not known whether services were actually received, the case was closed eight months before Ahsianea's death. "However the uncertainties of Ahsianea's case are resolved, she is more typical of thousands of needy children in the agency's purview who are at risk not because their parents are bad but because they are overwhelmed (NE 31)." Furthermore, her case is not atypical for poor families with medically fragile children whose needs can be met only by navigating the complicated medical establishment that even many who are sophisticated in its ways find difficult to do. Although it is not clear that social services could have prevented this child's death given the seriousness of her medical condition, it is clear that Ahsianea, her mother and siblings would have benefited from family services.

It is the intention of this book to examine public child welfare in the United States by using the example of family preservation. Family preservation has been promoted as an innovative service model, actually a collection of models, and as a philosophy of service delivery around which basic child welfare services can be organized. To be successful, it requires an eclectic repertoire of therapeutic skills as well as adjustments in the organization and administration of child welfare services.

References to family services in the United States can be found in the social work literature since its beginnings in the charity movement at the end of the nineteenth and beginning of the twentieth centuries; however, family, as the focus of service, has remained on the margins of child welfare practice subordinate to the dominant child saving theme. Family preservation advocates have managed to win its incorporation into public policy, into the social work textbooks, and into the practices of many social service agencies. But sadly for Ahsianea and her family, the public child welfare agencies that are responsible for abused and neglected children have been slow to embrace the family centered philosophy.

The twentieth century was remarkable on numerous counts. Developments in science and technology were nothing less than miraculous, and health and mental health care achieved levels of sophistication that increased the life span and quality of life of United States residents. The social history for children in the United States over this same period reveals a shift from conflicts over the working conditions of child laborers and high infant mortality rates (sixteen for every 100 urban births; Ehrenreich 1985, 21), to concerns about the social and psychological adjustment of children placed by working mothers in licensed day care facilities. Laws now prevent the exploitation of children in the marketplace, mandate education, provide food, shelter and medical assistance for qualified families, and give limited protection to children against abuse and neglect.

Although the number of social programs proliferated over this same period, qualitative advances in public programs designed to promote the welfare of dependent and neglected children have progressed slowly over the century. Our understanding of the psychology of family dynamics, the impact of social and economic factors on family functioning, the effects of environmental factors on the psychological and social development of children, and the professional skills that can be fruitfully applied to helping families overcome or adjust to the circumstances that bring about the need for official intervention, became much more sophisticated in the last half of the twentieth century. Similarly, we amassed a considerable body of knowledge about organizations and methods of organizing as we witnessed their proliferation in the interest of achieving social and economic objectives. We also experimented with different forms and structures of organizing, with new methods for managing our human and financial resources. However, the application of such knowledge, used to good effect in other service delivery systems, seems to have eluded the public child welfare agency.

In this chapter, we define family preservation services by giving examples of the prevailing models of practice and describe the public child welfare organization within which family preservation services operate. The structure and context of child welfare services must be understood if we are to comprehend the difficulties that program developers face when proposing changes, especially those that challenge existing methods, as family preservation services have consistently done. They must also be understood in order to examine the discourses of social work, family therapy, and public administration that influence child welfare practice.

Discourse refers not only to the language, the jargon and rhetoric that is peculiar to an area of study or practice, it also encompasses ideologies and behaviors. Discourses within a discipline are multiple. Our challenge is to show the inter-relatedness between multiple discourses while also considering the unique characteristics of each. There are at least three discourses that lead us to the place in social services practice that family preservation services occupy today. One is the social work specialization of child welfare, which has been linked initially and alternately over time to family casework. The importance of family casework to child welfare has found vocal advocates among those who are opposed to long-term foster care and the institutionalization of children. However, it is also contested by others as harmful to children and overly sympathetic to parents suspected of child abuse and neglect.

A second discourse is family therapy, a movement which found breath in the social work field with the work of Virginia Satir, a social worker in the Palo Alto group on the west coast, and with Carl Whitaker and Salvardor Minuchin at the Philadelphia Child Guidance Center, and Robert Gomberg and Nathan Ackerman at Jewish Family Services of New York, all in the 1950s and early 1960s. A third discourse, rarely discussed in this context, is public administration. The methods by which agencies organize and interact with one another, and the roles played by elected and appointed officials in their relations with local, state and federal governments in both developing and reacting to social policies, are significantly related to the success with which a public agency is able to achieve its service goals. Also a part of the public administration discourse is the community coordination and integration movement whose manager/administrator proponents, in the interest of efficiency, advocate shared responsibility for multi-problem clients across programmatic and functional disciplines. We will examine these three discourses in relation to family preservation practice and set the context for this examination below.

## *Family Preservation Defined*

Family preservation[1] is known by various other names including in-home family-based services, home-based services, family-centered services, and probably many others. More important than its name is its substance. The collection of programs that operate under these names and descriptors have the family as the locus of treatment and casework rather than the individual child. Attempts have been made in recent years to develop typologies of family preservation to clarify for policy makers and practitioners the programmatic differences that have evolved since the proliferation of these programs in the 1980s. These classifications range from the level of intensity in time spent with families, that is short-term, mid-range, and long-range treatment models, the theoretical approach used (including behavioral and systemic therapies), and the program characteristics of crisis intervention, home-based, and family treatment models (Nelson and Landsman 1992, 10-16). The Nelson-Landsman typology is the most inclusive since it incorporates setting, style, and substance of the family centered models operating today.

The crisis intervention model is very time-intensive in the short-term (6-8 weeks) with very low caseloads (2-6 family cases at a time). It uses behaviorist therapeutic approaches, and seeks to prevent or forestall a child's placement in foster care. The home-based models are similar to the crisis intervention model in that workers meet families in their homes; however, an ecological therapeutic approach derived from systems theory may be used. Caseloads tend to be slightly higher (6-10 family cases at a time) and treatment duration is a bit longer (2-6 months). The family treatment model may be home or office-based and emphasizes family systems theory along with structured family interviews, communications therapy, and with some families employs more than one therapist in interventions. These three models may co-exist in the same agency, public or private, or be a featured specialization of a single agency. They may incorporate an eclectic therapeutic philosophy including multiple treatment modalities, or a single, focused therapeutic model.

The family preservation construct is believed by its proponents to be one of the methods by which dysfunctional behaviors, both familial and organizational, may be reversed. However, the United States public child welfare system, where the family preservation approach can affect positively the most people, is a poor host. It is our premise that the structure and temperament of the organization are inhospitable to innovations that require substantive restructuring, and that it exhibits many of the dysfunctional characteristics that are attributed to the families that the child welfare system has been constituted to help. Otto Neurath compares the task of social scientists to repairing a leaky boat on an open sea (Cartwright 1996). Similarly, as much as one might wish it, it is not possible to begin a new child welfare system *tabula rasa;* the boat must be repaired while it is still afloat.

## The Public Child Welfare Bureaucracy

Before its recognition as a profession, social work claimed helping deserving poor children and widowed mothers through periods of extreme need as one of its principal activities. Orphanages were used freely to care for children whose parents were unable to provide for them financially. From the late nineteenth century, social workers have had a role in helping individual family members although the relationship has altered from time to time between close, personal involvement—like that nurtured by the friendly visitor volunteers—to a more formal professionalism[2]. The trend to professionalize was fostered by a desire to measure up to the emergent medical specialization with which the nascent social work profession sought to associate. Ehrenreich (1985, 123) notes that the psychiatric approach triumphed over the sociological approach to social casework in the 1920s. The individual as the focal point of treatment has long historical precedent in social work and remains stubbornly present today. Vestiges of the voluntary 'friendly visitor' approach still remain in some communities; however, the role that the social worker once played is now more often found among members of religious congregations and natural helping networks that are common to communities with few formal services.

There are elements of the family preservation philosophy in descriptions of family centered programs in the late 1940s through the early 1970s when family preservation began to take shape in its current form. Frances Scherz, a casework supervisor with Jewish Family and Community Service of Chicago defined family centered casework as ". . . based on an understanding of the social, physical, and emotional needs of the family as a unit for the purpose of helping the family members attain the best personal and social satisfaction of which they are capable (1953, 343)." Scherz notes that this form of casework was made possible in private family service agencies by their open door policies and their undifferentiated caseloads (349). Although her reference to personal and social satisfaction as treatment goals seem quaintly out of date, given the devastating nature of problems encountered in today's families, the cogency of her prescriptive focus remains relevant.

The flexibility that the private agency enjoyed is exceptional in the public agency. The bureaucratic model that was designed to legitimize the professional aims of child welfare work became a principal barrier to the use of family preservation models in public agencies. This bureaucratization is traced to the efficiency paradigm that began to emerge in the early part of the twentieth century when a shift occurred from cause to function and from the democratic to the bureaucratic organization. Lubove described the origins of the efficiency paradigm in social work as follows:

> The quest for efficiency and administrative technique in social agency operations paralleled the caseworker's efforts to reduce the range of intuition, subjectivity, and unpredictability in her own work. In both cases the volunteer introduced an element of uncertainty. Neither her livelihood nor social status depended upon conformity to agency policy or to the standards and procedures of professional casework. Volunteer service conflicted with the administrator's desire for rational, efficient organization and the social worker's identification with the agency as a vehicle for professional achieve- ment. (Lubove 1965, 161)

The efficiency sought as a means for legitimizing the professional social worker has had its consequences. Today's public child welfare agency has devolved into the organization type that sociologist, Max Weber feared in defining the pure bureaucratic type: bureaucratic efficiency has reduced the organization's capacity to respond to changes in its environment (Harman & Mayer 1986 79) and to its own clients. Furthermore, efficiency has become a bad joke in large urban agencies where the bureaucratic structure is the setting for chaos.

Programs for dependent children do not differ greatly from one another across state and local jurisdictions since most of their funds are federally derived with accompanying regulatory provisions that set the terms for their use. In general, agencies charged with the responsibility for dependent children are organized along traditional hierarchical lines, supervised by political appointees much the same as the organizations described by Willard in his 1924 survey of public welfare agencies. Headed by an administrator who may be a political appointee, and various departmental managers, direct client contact occurs at the bottom of the hierarchy by caseworkers organized into units. Units are headed by a casework supervisor who may, or may not, have a graduate degree in social work.

## Child Welfare Agency Functions

Client services tend to be organized by function. Intake, as it is generally known, is the front door through which requests for services are either accepted or rejected. Protective services are those in which investigations of allegations of abuse and neglect are conducted and determinations of the need for various services are made. These services may be provided directly or by connecting families with other service providers that offer counseling, parenting training, and day care, among others. Foster care placement includes recruiting, training and supervising foster families, and placing children with foster families, in group homes and residential institutions. Adoption involves recruiting, investigating, and approving prospective adopters, making adoptive placements, supervising these placements prior to legal finalization, and readying the adoption for finalization by the court. Services to juveniles (12-18 year olds) and services to disabled children (including health, mental health, and rehabilitative services) may be a part of these organizations, or as with other elements of the services described above, may be provided by other public agencies or contracted for with private organizations.

Contracting with private agencies is a commonly used method for extending to clients services that the public agency is unable or unwilling to provide. As contractors, private agencies have assumed the role of quasi-governmental entities, taking increasing responsibility for more and more basic casework services. Historically, these private agencies have been innovators in social services; however, many private providers have become extensions of the public agency as they have become dependent on government funds for their survival. The pressures of survival exacerbated by this dependency tend to promote risk-averse behaviors that inhibit innovation (Katz 1996, 271-272). As the number of private agencies that provide basic services proliferate, the number of professionals involved in determining a family's fate also increases. A single family with several children ranging in age from infant to teenager is likely to have multiple service providers often with conflicting service objectives. The involvement of multiple service providers creates time consuming service coordination challenges for caseworkers (or case managers) who, with seam-popping caseloads, may choose to apportion their limited time to those problems that seem most pressing, or to those families with whom they have established a relationship.

Some agencies have succeeded in meeting service coordination challenges by organizing teams of professionals in their communities that attempt to work together to set common goals for individual cases. However, these coordinating bodies require a serious commitment on the part of their members. Not only must they execute complex service plans, they must negotiate with contentious, often resistant systems (mental health, health, other social service providers, among others) whose members acknowledge the value of coordination in principle, but worry that collective decision making will encroach on their own and their agency's service prerogatives. Coordination does occur. However, impediments are present in most service communities, and overcoming them in the interest of each family's particular needs can be daunting. Certainly, a subtext of these efforts to coordinate services is to minimize attempts by clients to thwart the service provider's efforts to organize their lives and set limits on their behaviors.

Resources for helping families are not uniformly available in many service communities in the United States. Rural and financially pressed urban areas may be seriously resource poor. Nevertheless, living in a service rich area does not insure that resources will be available when a family needs them. For example, mental health services are notoriously difficult to obtain and day care is scarce to name but two. The numbers of families that do without needed services are unknown. It is apparent, however, that in many of our communities basic service needs are consistently ignored. This is in part because the political will is not there to provide sufficient resources to make meaningful assistance possible, and in part because the system, itself, is overly complex and resistant to change.

Whether or not a family gets help seems to be largely the luck of the draw. Several studies (Rossi 1992a; Littell and Schuerman 1995) that examine family preservation have suggested that family preservation casework may actually increase the possibility of a child's placement in foster care. This claim is based on the observation that when sufficient time is spent in understanding a family's problems, behaviors that pose an imminent danger to a child are recognized, and the child's removal may be more prudent, at least in the short term, than in-home therapy. Contrary to detractors' arguments, family preservation appears to be a safer bet for preventing child abuse than traditional (minimal) casework services. When a system is so overburdened that it can no longer achieve its stated service objectives, it is in danger of iatrogenesis, the term used in medicine to describe doctor-induced harm. It may be applied to caseworkers who, in an overburdened social service system, escalate dangerous family tensions by intervening but then failing to offer treatment.

The following vignette is an adaptation of a suspected child maltreatment (protective service) case in a mid-sized urban agency. It is typical of the routine tasks involved in the majority of cases. This appears to be a case of child neglect involving neither physical nor sexual abuse. We ask the reader to imagine at which junctures in the case other decisions might have been made to obviate the need for placing five young children in foster care. All names are fictitious.

## The T. Family

### Day One

The call came from the resident on duty at Children's Hospital to the Children's Services Agency 24-hour on-call intake worker at 5:35 a.m. The resident reported that a young mother with an 8-week old, dehydrated, lethargic infant had come to the emergency room an hour earlier. The child's mother seemed disoriented to the resident who suspected the mother of drug use and child neglect. As a mandated reporter (someone who by virtue of their professional position is required by law to report cases of suspected child abuse or neglect), he was submitting the findings of his initial examination. After quizzing the resident for basic information required on her intake form, the intake worker indicated that someone from the agency would appear within the next forty-eight hours. Since the infant was being admitted to the pediatric ward and her safety was assured, an immediate response was unnecessary. The resident, having discharged his responsibility, was satisfied with this response. The intake worker logged the call and copied the initial intake form for processing by the protective service workers arriving at 8:30 a.m. for their regular day shift.

\* \* \* \*

Priscilla T. had had a difficult delivery. Her baby was small at birth, weighing just over five pounds. At twenty-five years old, she now had five children, and her husband, Carlo, who was the baby's father and the father of three of her other children, was out of work again. She had sought prenatal care only intermittently since to reach the clinic required two bus transfers. Her mother and two sisters, who might have helped with her children and lived only a few blocks away, were not on speaking terms with Priscilla. Taking the children on the bus ride to the clinic was exhausting. Priscilla and her husband had grown up in the neighborhood where they now lived. Although they knew almost everyone around them, she kept to herself. Carlo met with buddies from high school and several of the jobs he'd had. However, he rarely brought them home—a two bedroom apartment in a deteriorating housing project.

When this baby was born, it took Priscilla longer to recover. The older children were demanding, and Carlo wasn't interested in helping out. Priscilla hadn't liked the idea of nursing her baby but the nurse in the hospital pressed her to do so. She tried, even though Carlo teased her. A visiting nurse came by the house a few days after Priscilla and Carlo brought the new baby home. She gave her some formula samples but encouraged her to continue nursing the baby. After one visit, the nurse had not returned.

* * * *

The twenty-five protective services workers arriving for work that morning met briefly with their supervisors to review their active cases and to be assigned the new investigation requests that had come in the previous night. There were sixteen calls that required investigation, which is about average for a weeknight. The department manager had called a staff meeting for 10:00 a.m. to review a new policy directive from the agency administrator; the meeting was expected to last about an hour. Each of the protective service workers had active caseloads of 20-25—the new calls were distributed among them. Infant T. was assigned to Anne Michaels. She had been with the Children's Services Agency for four years and was considered a competent investigator, although most of her training was on the job. With a bachelor's degree in sociology from a local university, Anne went through the agency's standard new-worker training program. She noted that in each of the three newly assigned cases, the children were safe for the time being, since they were either in the hospital, or in the emergency shelter facility.

With her supervisor's approval, Anne scheduled interviews for that afternoon with four of the cases pending from two days ago, and spent the morning making follow-up phone calls, and doing the paperwork necessary to transfer several completed investigations to the family service department. Most uncomplicated investigations, that is, those in which the police or physicians had already made a preliminary determination that abuse or neglect had occurred, took about four hours to complete, including travel time. Complaints from the public, usually a neighbor or relative, could take longer, particularly if the child was in school and there were several adults involved.

The agency's administrator had received complaints from someone in the mayor's office who said that agency workers were taking too long to investigate abuse calls. The agency's regulations required that emergencies be dealt with within twenty-four hours, and that responses to all other calls should be completed within thirty-six to forty-eight hours. The protective service workers were good about responding to the emergencies within the required time, but many of their non-emergency cases took up to a week to complete.

\* \* \* \*

Jack Parsons had been appointed administrator of the Children's Services Agency three months earlier after the previous administrator had been fired. There had been the death of a child who was an active case with the agency, and the ensuing clamor resulting from a series of investigative newspaper articles, made it possible for the mayor to get rid of an unpopular agency head. Parsons was selected for the job, his first as head of an agency, by the mayor for whom Parsons had worked as a legislative aid for several years. He considered this an opportunity to prove his value as an administrator and hoped to head up a more important agency in the local government hierarchy in the not too distant future.

On arriving at the Children's Services Agency he was appalled at the physical condition of the buildings and at the uniform silence of the supervisors at their first meeting together. However, in his separate meetings with the managers and supervisors, each made clear to him their complaints about the operation of the other units, and not infrequently, the work of their fellow managers and supervisors. Rumors, many contradictory, raced through the ranks about the changes he was expected to make, and he received calls daily for the first few weeks from the agency's contractors who wanted to make sure he understood the importance of their contributions to the agency's work.

He was in the midst of putting together the next fiscal year's budget and was irritated with the complaint from the mayor's office since he knew the protective services department was doing its best and that the new budget had no room in it for additional caseworkers. Nevertheless, he had instructed the department manager to meet with the caseworkers to discuss ways to move the investigations along more rapidly.

* * * *

Priscilla had noticed that her baby wasn't gaining weight; she was constantly fussing and never seemed to get her fill when nursing. On this night, the third day that the baby had had a cold, Priscilla waited for Carlo to come home so that she could take her into the emergency room to see a doctor. He arrived around 2:00 a.m. drunk; they argued, he'd hit her, and she'd smoked marijuana to calm her nerves before calling a taxi to take her to the hospital. On her arrival, an emergency room doctor examined her baby. He asked her several questions that she found difficult to answer then told her he would be admitting the baby because she was too sick to take home. Priscilla told him that she had to get back to her other children and left. Upon returning home, Priscilla, exhausted, went to bed. Carlo was asleep on the sofa and the children were asleep in front of the television.

* * * *

Anne Michaels telephoned the hospital that morning to determine the status of Baby T. and was told by the pediatric resident that the baby was being treated, that the mother had left and that they didn't want to release the baby to her when she returned. She then called the foster care supervisor to request an emergency foster home placement for Baby T. The hospital admission form indicated that the family had no telephone, so she planned to visit them the following morning and proceeded to work through the cases she had scheduled for that day. She had attended the staff meeting that morning which she found depressing. She and her colleagues took these complaints in stride since they knew there was little more that could be done to expedite cases. The foster care supervisor left word for Michaels that St. Mary's Children's Home had an emergency foster home placement ready for Baby T. A nurse on the pediatric ward had also left word that the baby was to be discharged the following day.

* * * *

Priscilla awoke at 11:00 AM to find Carlo gone, the kids screaming at each other and no food in the house. Carlo hadn't sent her five and six year old daughters to school where they could have had breakfast, so she dressed them and their two and four year old brothers and, with her last four dollars and remaining food stamps, walked to the store for bread and milk. Without money to get to the hospital, she did not know how her baby was doing and was unaware that Children's Services had been called. She asked around on the street for Carlo, but no one had seen him since the night before. Priscilla returned home with her children to wait. Carlo returned home that evening to find the usual chaos. Priscilla was yelling at the kids, there was no dinner waiting. He brought beer with him and proceeded to drink it. Priscilla wanted to go to the hospital but he talked her out of it saying he was short of cash and didn't want to spend what little he had on cab fare. They fought until he lost his temper and left.

## Day Two

Anne Michaels called in to say she was taking a personal day; her six year old son was at home with the flu. Marion O'Reilly, her supervisor, also supervised seven other protective services workers. It was not unusual that at least one of them was out sick or on leave at any given time, and she tried her best to fill in when this occurred. It was against agency policy to place a child in foster care without first interviewing a parent, if a parent could be found, but in Baby T's case the hospital had called twice and an emergency foster home was waiting. The agency was permitted to make emergency placements for up to three days without a court order, and this appeared to be such a case. Marion called the foster care supervisor at St. Mary's asking that she send her foster care worker to the hospital to retrieve Baby T. This done, she put a note in Baby T's file and placed it on Anne Michaels' desk ordering Anne to find Baby T's mother as soon as she returned to work.

* * * *

Priscilla was becoming anxious. She had gotten a fairly good night's sleep with the baby in the hospital, the two older children had gone to school, and Carlo had borrowed money from somewhere and left her enough to buy more groceries and pay for transportation to the hospital. Her neighbor had grudgingly allowed her to use his telephone to call the hospital, but the nurse with whom she spoke said only that the baby was doing well. With the boys in tow, she took the bus this time and arrived at the hospital around 10:30 in the morning. Once there, she had difficulty finding someone to talk with her; they wouldn't allow her children to accompany her to the ward, there was no one to leave them with, so she left them in the waiting area alone.

When she arrived on the ward, the nurse and the social worker from St. Mary's Children's Home were preparing the baby for discharge. Once it became clear to her that her baby was being taken by the social worker, Priscilla became angry and demanded that the baby be returned to her. The social worker then called the Children's Services Agency for instructions and, finding neither O'Reilly nor Michaels there, spoke with the protective services department manager. After locating and reading the file, the manager instructed another protective services worker to go immediately to the hospital to determine what must be done. By the time she arrived, the situation with Priscilla had escalated. The duty clerk in the waiting area had notified security that two children had been abandoned there. Priscilla had been taken to a hospital social worker's office accompanied by the St. Mary's worker where she continued to argue with them. Assessing the immediate circumstances, the protective service worker instructed the St. Mary's social worker to take the child. She explained to the distraught mother that the placement was necessary until an investigation of the baby's home could be conducted and a determination made that the baby would be safe there. She told Priscilla to go home, that a social worker would visit her the following day. Reluctantly, Priscilla left for the waiting area to retrieve her sons only to be confronted by two security guards who threatened to call the police. Taking the boys, Priscilla went home.

## Day Three

Anne Michaels returned to work to find a stack of messages marked urgent from the hospital social worker, the St. Mary's social worker, her supervisor, and the protective service worker who had met Priscilla at the hospital. Added to the seven new cases that had appeared on her desk that morning, she wished that she hadn't come back. After returning their calls and getting blamed for a situation that they thought she could have prevented, Anne got into her car and headed to Priscilla's home. There she found the family in confusion and disarray. Carlo was berating Priscilla for involving them with social services, the children were cowering in the bedroom, and Priscilla was alternately crying and cursing.

When Carlo turned his anger on Ms. Michaels, she left to call for police assistance. When the police arrived twenty minutes later, Carlo had already left. While they remained in the apartment, Anne talked with the older children and with Priscilla. Anne noted that the house was dirty, food had been left out and had attracted flies and roaches, there was little food in the refrigerator and cupboards, the children were dirty, and although quiet now, Priscilla was clearly emotionally distraught and appeared physically ill. Anne told Priscilla that the baby could not come home until Anne could be certain that she would be properly cared for. She said that she would transfer the case to a family service worker immediately, so that the family could get the help they would need to make the baby's return possible. She then left with the police.

Upon returning to the agency, Anne completed the paper work to transfer the case to the Family Services

Department, and completed the request for a court order for temporary placement of Baby T. She placed both on her supervisor's desk for approval. Marion O'Reilly was quick to act on the case transfer since she'd received word from her manager indicating that news of the scene at Children's Hospital had already reached the agency administrator.

## Day Six

Patty Baker was assigned the Baby T. file on Friday just before quitting time. She read the file, called St. Mary's to determine the status of Baby T., who, she was told, had been transferred to a non-emergency foster home and was making progress there. Anne Michaels had obtained the court order for placement without difficulty. She saw nothing more in the file about police involvement with the family and determined to visit them first thing on Monday morning.

When she arrived at the T's apartment, the situation was dire. Priscilla was clearly ill; the children had apparently not eaten for some time, and Carlo had not returned since the day Anne Michaels had been there. Using her car phone, Patty called an ambulance for Priscilla, and the agency for another caseworker and infant seat—she had only one with her. Patty and the back-up caseworker placed the four children in their cars and followed the ambulance to the hospital. She requested that her supervisor identify one or more emergency foster homes for the four children once they'd been examined by a doctor and released. Priscilla was admitted to the hospital with a high fever, apparent malnutrition and dehydration. The children were pronounced well enough to leave after the doctor's examination, and were subsequently separated with the two older children going to the emergency shelter, and the two younger children to emergency foster homes.

## Day Eight

Priscilla remained in the hospital for three days during which time court orders were obtained for the temporary placement of her remaining four children. In the meantime, Patty had learned the names and addresses of Priscilla's mother and sisters and had met with each of them to determine whether a family member could take in Priscilla's children and help her when she was discharged from the hospital. Priscilla's mother agreed to take the two older children, but the two sisters were unwilling to help. Patty called the visiting nurse agency and was told that a nurse could visit Priscilla in her home only once after her discharge from the hospital since they had a waiting list and were understaffed. She then called the foster care supervisor requesting that Priscilla's mother be investigated and certified as a foster parent; she was told that it could be done within the next two weeks. In the meantime, the girls were moved from the shelter to emergency foster homes pending their grandmother's foster care certification.

Priscilla left the hospital weak and depressed. She took a taxi to her empty apartment with the money the social worker had given her. She had an appointment to see Patty Baker at her office the following day but didn't think she could make it. She remained in the apartment alone.

## Day Nine

Priscilla failed to appear for her appointment with Patty Baker, who recorded the failure in Priscilla's file.

## Day Twenty-two

Patty had tried several times to contact Priscilla to no avail. Since there was no telephone, she had to go to the T. family's home. On the first two visits, no one answered the door. On her third visit, a neighbor told her that Priscilla no longer lived there. She contacted Priscilla's mother, who had just been certified to take the older children, but she did not know Priscilla's whereabouts. Patty notified the foster families and the court that Priscilla had disappeared, and that Carlo was not to be found.

## Month Three

Priscilla reappeared at the Children's Services Agency requesting that her children be returned to her. She said that she was living with a friend, working as a waitress and had seen the two oldest children at her mother's home, but she didn't know where the others were. Patty Baker phoned Priscilla's mother who admitted that Priscilla had been there, but had not thought it necessary to notify the agency. With Priscilla's reappearance, Patty began the series of visits that would ultimately lead to the return of all five children to their mother six months later. Unfortunately, this episode in the experience of the T. family was only the first of several over the years to come.

## Risk Avoidance

Public agency employees are caught between the desire to help their clients and the desire for relief from a constant flow of new clients, and from old, closed cases that reappear with predictable frequency. The child welfare caseworker can only be sure that a case will be closed when a family's children are emancipated—but even some of these cases are multigenerational as when children of former clients have children of their own and become clients themselves. She can look upon these types of cases as social failures and treat them as hopeless— or with the limited tools given to her by the agency and the community, and her own wits, she can see each new problem as a challenge.

Most of the caseworkers we have known are aware that with a few more resources they could experience the satisfaction of closure more frequently. Since public child welfare agencies are 'residual' in nature their control over the selection of clients is limited[3]. The only means by which public agencies may be selective is in narrowing the criteria that define what constitutes abuse and neglect. Of course, they do so at their peril. When a poorly investigated abuse or neglect complaint results in the death of a child, everyone in the agency is affected, as well they should be.

Public criticism by officials in the courts and schools, and among health and mental health care providers, other service organizations and advocacy groups increase the stress on the public child welfare agency. This unsought after attention by the community also contributes to the view that the agency's critics are predatory, lying in wait to expose any and every misstep. A way to avoid criticism from the community is to be risk-averse. Innovation is associated with risk, and fear of failure and censure reinforces risk-averse behavior.

Innovative programs like family preservation services literally push up against rock-hard systems. Administrators and caseworkers are simply too overwhelmed with the day-to-day press of work to think seriously about learning new skills, or making substantive changes in the work environment. New ways of working require time to learn new methods and design new procedures. Time for learning and reflection in the child welfare environment is rare. When innovations do break through an agency's professional barriers, administrative and bureau-cratic impediments must be overcome if they are to have any chance of succeeding, particularly if an innovation requires additional resources and substantial revisions in accepted practices.

There are external barriers as well. One such barrier is the family court judge who, in exercising the court's considerable influence, can successfully frustrate an agency's attempts to change. Furthermore, the organization that risks change may climb the mountain only to be pushed back down again by an election, new agency leadership, or budget cut backs. To those who toil in the child welfare system it must seem that every aspect of the agency's environment is dedicated to these two extremes: complaining that the system must change, and thwarting change at every turn.

## Child Welfare's Workers

Many public agencies are handicapped by an unfortunate lack of workers with diagnostic skills and therapeutic expertise. Caseworkers bring varying degrees of educational and professional experience to managing cases and providing face-to-face interaction with parents and children. Efforts have been made by schools of social work and the professional organizations that set standards for the field to advance the professional education and training of practicing social workers. However, two trends have made staffing public child welfare agencies difficult. First, the federal funding (Title IV-B of the Social Security Act) used historically by schools of social work for training people already working in the field has steadily declined in recent years; and secondly, a desire to work in public child welfare by students in schools of social work has given way to a preference for private practice. The reputation of public child welfare agencies for high caseloads and poor working conditions is, no doubt, a contributing factor in the choice students make.

The constituency of the National Association of Social Workers is the professionally trained social worker. The public agency worker with a degree in another discipline is not permitted full membership in the organization. Furthermore, the national organization continues to lobby for restricted use of the term 'social worker' to those with a degree in the field (NASW 1999)[4]. Although some professional social workers have lobbied to license workers through state regulatory mechanisms, they have been largely unsuccessful. States that are faced with worker shortages and a need to fill low-wage, entry-level positions, particularly in rural areas, are tempted to alter state hiring practices to accept those with minimal educational qualifications.

When state legislatures and state administrative apparatuses refuse to acknowledge the need to employ professionally trained social workers in their public child welfare agencies, it is testament to the lack of importance placed on the needs of public agency clients. It is also testament to an apparent shortcoming in the social work discipline that it has been unsuccessful in maintaining its professional presence in the one area, child welfare, which has historically been under its purview. Meanwhile, lacking time, skills, and expertise to diagnose and treat family problems, public agency caseworkers with large caseloads place children in foster homes as insurance against the nightmare of a dead or maimed child.

The instability of the public agency workforce, evidenced by astonishingly high employee turnover impedes efforts to positively affect family functioning, a requisite for maintaining an intact family (See Schorr 2000, for more on current trends in worker turnover rates). Maintaining a stable workforce is hampered by excessive caseloads and their attendant pressures, low wages relative to the job's expectations, a lack of preparedness for the tasks required, a low-trust environment inside the child welfare agency, a distrustful community of professional colleagues outside the agency, and a repeatedly confirmed belief that caseworkers are impotent to help families resolve the multiple problems that bring them to the agency. When a caseworker leaves the

agency, her caseload is either divided up among those who remain
behind, adding to their burden, or is handed over to her replacement
who may not arrive for several months or more. In the meantime,
whatever casework was occurring on that caseload, ceases.

By virtue of their legal, custodial mandates and fiduciary
responsibilities, public child welfare agencies act *in loco parentis* for
hundreds of thousands of children in the United States, over half a
million of whom are in foster care. Given the problems we describe, it
is safe to say that the state makes a poor substitute for a parent, even for
a parent who is considered to be incompetent. Yet the processes
involved in determining who is, and who is not a candidate for out-of-
home placement and the relationship that these decisions have on
contractual agreements established with private service providers have
a significant bearing on the fates of these children and their families, a
point that we will discuss shortly.

As noted, over-burdened child welfare systems receive attention
periodically in the popular press when a child dies under an agency's
supervision. Caseworkers are blamed for their failure to intervene—
recriminations abound. However, the public outrage is invariably
temporary, assuaged with promises of remedies designed to quiet
criticism. In 1971, researcher Ludwig Geismar claimed that the
unwillingness of social welfare agencies to scientifically evaluate their
product was attributable to their monopolistic position in the
community. Neither their survival nor their growth depend on the
quality of the services rendered since survival is assured (11). It is true
that the agency is monopolistic and, while its existence is guaranteed,
community support is not. Rarely are the barriers that are endemic to
the ubiquitous bureaucracy examined or removed. It is more likely that
attention to these systemic problems take the form of new leadership,
new rules and reorganizations that further demoralize an embattled
workforce.

The child welfare agency exemplifies a collision of discourses. For
example, one discourse involves the language of social work adapted
by untrained caseworkers that have been abandoned by their putative
social work mentors, and another is the language of administration that
prizes bureaucratic efficiency and political expedience over client
welfare. Both discourses coexist in a highly charged, stressful environment that perpetuates the organization's dysfunctional behaviors while
appearing to outsiders—much as the agency's clients appear—as
irrational and hopeless in the face of change.

## The Children

On any given day in fiscal year 1999, 568,000 children were in foster care, an 8,000 child increase from the 1998 (the fiscal year is from October 1, 1998 to September 30, 1999). During the last half of the 1999 fiscal year, 143,000 entered and 122,000 children exited foster care. Of the children in foster care on any given day, 36 percent were White Non-Hispanic, 42 percent were Black Non-Hispanic, 15 percent were Hispanic and 7 percent were of other races and ethnic origins. The median age was 10.1 years old. Over half (52 percent) were boys[5].

Collecting the data that would give us a clear picture of the non-foster care service population of the child welfare system is much more difficult. The most recent study that reported systematically collected service data was published in 1994 by the U.S. Department of Health and Human Services. As of March 1, 1994,[6] there were an estimated 999,100 children in 577,000 families with open cases in public child welfare agencies. Forty-one percent were African-American children, 11 percent Hispanic, 46 percent White, and 4 percent of other races or ethnic groups. The average age was 8.5 years. Four percent were less than one year old, 24 percent were between 1 and 4 years, 25 percent, between five and eight years, and 20 percent each between nine and twelve, and thirteen and sixteen years. Seven percent were seventeen or older. Almost half of the open cases (48 percent) involved children with disabling conditions that included developmental disabilities, emotional disturbance, learning disabilities, and hearing, speech or sight impairment, among others. Of substantiated cases (a legal determination was made), 35 percent were reported as physical or emotional abuse, 12 percent as sexual abuse, and 54 percent as lack of supervision and physical neglect.

According to the same report, 28 percent of all the white children, 40 percent of the Hispanic children, and 56 percent of the African American children in the system were in foster care. (Not to be confused with the percentages of children by race *in* foster care reported above.) African-American children are represented in greater numbers in foster care than White or Hispanic children; however, African-American children are also more likely to be placed with family members (kinship care) than are white and Hispanic children.

Sixty-six percent of children went into foster care placement within the first three months of case opening. The average length of time in non-kinship foster care placements for African-American children is thirty-three months, for Hispanic children, thirty-five months, and for white children, eighteen months. Eighty-three percent of children in kinship foster care (the foster parent is a relative) and 59 percent of children in non-kinship placements experienced one placement; 10 percent of children in kinship care, and 33 percent of non-kinship placements experienced more than 1 placement (U.S. Dept. of Health and Human Services, Children's Bureau, 1994). The report takes special notice that, "a differential [by race] service delivery system exists (8-5)". It reports further that although the Third National Incidence Study on Child Abuse and Neglect (NIS-3) does not identify racial or ethnic differences in maltreatment incidence, it clearly indicates that differential attention by race occurs somewhere in the process of referral, investigation, and service allocation (7-22).

All too familiar to agency workers, is what we call the 'foster placement spiral'. This occurs when a child out-grows or out-stays his welcome in the foster home in which he was placed (a foster family that keeps only infants, is an example). A child may experience multiple foster homes before reaching an age when willing foster parents can no longer be found. He is then placed in a group home or residential institution. When a child's behavior or medical problems are too difficult to manage, restrictive institutional placements are often viewed as the only alternative until he reaches his eighteenth birthday and is emancipated. This marks the end of the placement spiral. A child who experiences multiple placements also experiences multiple health care providers, schools, and social workers. Continuity of any sort is difficult, if not impossible to maintain. It results in gaps in a child's education, medical, dental and mental health care, and more pointedly, in the nurturing relationships that most of us believe are important to the development of healthy, well-adjusted adults. At the same time, the families of these children are abandoned by the system with little hope of regaining their children before the latter reach an age when they can return home on their own.

## Contracted Services

The relationships forged between public agencies and their private counterparts also have a part to play in this process. The delegation of responsibility for a child's well being to a private agency may be a mixed blessing. The private agency may be able to offer more, and possibly better services because they have some control over their caseload size. They enjoy more structural flexibility; however, they are also free to wash their hands of a child whose problems they cannot, or prefer not, to deal with. New York City's child welfare system is an example. Most of the city's services to children have been contracted to religious-affiliated agencies, and the bureaucratic morass that has resulted is legendary among child welfare professionals (O'Connor 2001, A23).

In addition, certain aspects of the contractual relationship may actually create incentives to keep children in foster care rather than to work towards a child's reunification with her family. For example, when a private residential agency's contract is tied to a per diem rate, the agency has an incentive to maintain a full house since its financial stability depends on the number of beds that are continuously filled. This 'per diem' arrangement also exerts subtle pressures on caseworkers and the courts to place children rather than to work with families towards reunification. Private agency administrators may prefer the stability that fixed annual contracts can provide, yet may be unable to convince public agency administrators and policy makers of the utility of fixed contracts as a foster care prevention strategy.

The conflicting goals that bedevil the public child welfare agency are a problem for the residential facility contractor, as well. Working with the families of children in their care can be disruptive. Emotionally charged meetings between parents and children create tensions which disrupt the daily routine in the residential facility and cause problems for institutional childcare workers. Childcare workers tend to be poorly compensated,[7] with training limited to behavioral management techniques, a euphemism for techniques designed to physically subdue unruly children. It is in the agency's interest, therefore, to resist innovations that disrupt the daily routine, particularly when they cannot be certain that policy changes will be sustained by the public agency on which they depend for referrals. These interagency relationships are a rarely examined but an equally important element to our understanding of a child welfare system. The mantle of silence that envelops the public agency-private contractor relationship is maintained for good reasons.

The large public agency can no longer manage its caseloads alone; it must rely on private contractors. And private contractors, on whose boards of directors sit well-placed, politically influential citizens, must not operate at a financial loss. In order to 'fire' a non-compliant contractor, the public agency must have substitute service options ready (a particularly difficult problem when the service is foster or institutional care). As Steven Cohen, the administrator who oversaw contracting relations with New York City's child placement agencies in the early 1980s, observed, "You can't regulate anything when the suppliers control the market (Bernstein 1998, 26 NE)."

## The Court

We have mentioned that the court plays a significant role in placement choices. Federal child welfare law requires that judges review and recommend services for families and children for whom the agency has a custodial relationship. The term 'iron triangle' has been used in reference to the strong, interdependent relationships among federal agencies, congressional committees and subcommittees, and interest groups. This metaphor is equally applicable to the relationships that exist among the public child welfare agency, the court, and private contractors at the local level. It is a relationship that was masterminded by child welfare advocates whose distrust of the public agency led to the inclusion of judicial oversight in national child welfare legislation passed in 1980 (Public Law 96-272).[8] Judicial oversight was seen as a method for insuring that neither the court nor the child welfare agency allows children to languish in foster care. However, it is not unusual to find the court extending its reach into decisions that, it could be argued, should be left to agency workers. Caseworkers often contend with judges who are disinterested, derisive of the agency and its workers, and patronizing with workers and families. This may be understandable when a judge is faced with daily doses of confused, incompletely researched cases, new workers, and unhappy witnesses.

We know judges of good will who have made extraordinary efforts to address children's needs against the odds. However, family court also is at times staffed by judges who would prefer higher status assignments, and who suffer barbs from their peers and attorneys for their work in 'kiddie court'. Workers complain that judges tend to deal more harshly with poor, minority families than with those who are middle class and white. Nevertheless, in the 1997 Adoption and Family Safe Families Act[9] the court continues to have a prominent role in case planning decisions.

## Conclusion

We have suggested that the difficulties encountered in integrating family preservation into public child welfare services have to do with the presence of overwhelming mandates imposed on the system to guarantee the safety of abused an neglected children: first, to find alternative caretakers for them when it is determined that their families cannot care for them, and secondly, to find adoptive families when return home is unworkable. A system that is already overwhelmed lacks the psychological space to learn new service philosophies and therapeutic techniques. Furthermore, public child welfare caseworkers are poorly prepared for such challenges, and lack support for risk-taking from their colleagues and associates in the broader service community. Impeding the success of prevention programs like family preservation are issues of a political nature—particularly, as we have noted, when public agency policies threaten programs and prerogatives favored by influential citizens, agency executives and board members. Compounding these problems is the danger that the child welfare system is losing its strongest traditional advocates—that is, professional social workers, schools of social work, and social work's professional organizations, to a preference for conducting individual and family therapy in the relative safety and comfort of private practice.

Although this description of the public child welfare system is not a flattering one, we recognize that many, perhaps most, of the workers who toil in child welfare agencies are good-hearted people with a genuine desire to do what they can for their clients. We are also aware of many selfless people who have dedicated their careers to unsnarling red tape in behalf of 'their' families. The system about which we write is not composed of villains, although there is something seriously wrong with it, and it is this to which we wish to draw attention. In the chapters that follow, we will argue that the multiple discourses that operate in the child welfare space have resulted in a cacophony of voices, and that the resulting discord has muted the children's voices, and in so doing, has led to the orphaning of child welfare.

---

**Notes**

[1] Not to be confused with family preservation described by M.B. Katz, *In the Shadow of the Poorhouse: A Social History of Welfare in America.* (New York: Basic Books, 1996) as a doctrine designed to keep children with their parent(s) during the Progressive movement at the turn of the twentieth century. Katz suggests that the social consequences of this doctrine were to turn the new found "pricelessness" of children into the powerlessness of both women and children (p.130).

[2] Hancock, B.L. & Pelton, L. (1989) give a brief history of "home visiting" as a function of social work practice, beginning with the Charity Organization Society (COS) movement that flourished in the latter half of the nineteenth century, in "Home Visits: History and Functions" *Social Casework* 70(1):21-27.

[3] A. L. Schorr (2000) uses the term 'residual' to describe the historically limited-mission given to child welfare agencies, which was to care for children who were separated from their parents for other than financial reasons. In practice though, the children cared for by the child welfare system are those for whom there is no other recourse — the 'residue.'

[4] The National Association of Social Workers (NASW) states that only about one-third of all professional social workers are employed by federal, state or local governments, and that only about 28% of child welfare workers have a Bachelors or Masters of Social Work. NASW Internet Web site. (http://www.naswdc.org/), January 1999.

[5] The states are mandated to report certain foster care and adoption data to the federal government's AFCARS data collection program. The data is reported on the National Clearing House on Child Abuse and Neglect web site: (April 23, 2001). http://www.calib.com/nccanch/pubs/factsheets/foster.cfm

[6] 1994 data is used for two reasons: it does not differ substantially from later estimates (1997 DHHS), and the methodology that Westat, Inc., used for gathering it is more reliable, in our view, than self-reported data produced for the DHHS Internet Web sites.

[7] Median hourly wage for childcare workers in the US was $6.12 in 1998, compared with $10.35 for all workers. (Kids Count Data, Annie E. Casey Foundation: http://www.aecf.org.)

[8] Public Law 96-272 is the Adoption Opportunities and Child Welfare Act that was passed by the U.S. Congress in 1980 and was considered landmark child welfare legislation because it focused on a time-limited foster care review by the court, and emphasized the adoption of 'waiting' children.

[9] The Adoption and Safe Families Act was passed by the U.S. Congress in 1997, reaffirming Congressional and Administration support for the adoption of children who cannot return home in a reasonable time.

# Chapter 2

## Alternatives to Foster Care

### Introduction

Everyone who has worked in child welfare can remember a child who has experienced multiple foster care placements—I recall a shy little girl with dark blond hair and pale blue eyes who, by age seven had experienced twenty-six placements. She was eventually adopted by an older couple without children since it was felt that Sarah could not share her parents with others. Kareem, a diabetic, was eleven years old when I first met him. After multiple foster homes, he was in his third group home placement having learned to get his way by threatening to eat forbidden foods he pilfered from the other children. The group home staff was not prepared to handle a child with medical problems of this nature. When their frustrations with him exceeded their patience, a 30-day termination of service notice was given and the search for a new residence began.

Sharon was sexually molested and physically abused by several of her mother's boyfriends over most of her life. The descriptions of the abuse she endured will haunt us all as long as we have memory. At thirteen she was sent to a co-ed residential treatment center with a therapeutic program for sexually abused adolescents. After only three months at the institution, Sharon's caseworker was notified that Sharon was pregnant and would need a placement in a maternity facility. Placed with her baby at a new program designed for teen mothers,

Sharon would not conform to the rules. Her baby was placed in foster care. Sharon never remained anywhere very long, running away at the first opportunity. At sixteen, Sharon told the judge she wanted to live with her mother. At their wits end, her caseworkers concurred, and Sharon went home.

This chapter is about foster care and some of the alternatives suggested as options to it. Two initiatives that were proposed in the late 1960s were supposed to benefit children like Sarah, Kareem and Sharon—children who experienced multiple foster care placements. The first initiative was the adoption of so-called special needs (older, handicapped and non-white) children. The second was a case management strategy called permanency planning. A third initiative, at the time called in-home family-based services, was similar to a program that had been in place for twenty years in St. Paul, Minnesota. The St. Paul Family Centered Project shared a number of similarities with several of the new programs begun in the early 1970s in Iowa and Wisconsin. It is reviewed here as an example of clashing discourses— in this case among practitioners, administrator and consultants. The cacophonous voices of the professional community drown out the voices the program was designed to serve.

In 1974, Congress passed the Child Abuse Prevention and Treatment Act (Public Law 93-247) that encouraged the reporting and treatment of abused and neglected children, prompting a significant increase in the number of children entering foster care in the early 1970s.[1] Although this was not the first time that an exploding foster care population worried child welfare professionals, the numbers following passage of the child abuse legislation were astounding, and pointed out with sharp clarity the need to help an overwhelmed child welfare system. This precipitated three distinct programs. The first sought to expedite the adoption of children of all ages and circumstances where hitherto, adoptability was circumscribed by age, race, and health to infants, generally white, of readily verifiable lineage.

The second was called permanency planning and signified a renewed emphasis on the temporary nature of foster care and the need to make time-limited plans to return children to their families or, barring this possibility, to encourage their adoption. The third initiative, in-home family-based services, was designed to help families remedy the problems that brought them to the attention of the social service agency through the use of therapeutic techniques, and to prevent, whenever possible, placing children in foster care. Although each of these initiatives emphasized elements that were already implicit in child welfare practice, it had become clear, given the growing number of children who were stalled in the system, that specific initiatives were needed to promote their widespread use.

The foster care system had devolved into little more than a repository for youngsters whose parents had given up on them, were without the resources to afford medical and mental health services for them, or were judged to be incompetent to parent them. With the advent of child abuse legislation, children were being removed from their families ostensibly to the safety of loving foster families. Unfortunately, little was known about the emotional scars that accompanied physical abuse, and children who had been abused at the hands of a parent, were now being abused at the hands of a foster parent. Federal funds for foster care were distributed to states under the IV-B section of the Social Security Act. These funds were not capped, making foster care placement an attractive alternative to hiring caseworkers and further solidifying the role in child welfare of the private foster care industry which employs well-compensated executives and marginal wage caretakers.

## Alternatives to Foster Care

The first of these alternatives, the adoption of children with special needs, encountered only minimal resistance from public agencies once it became evident that adoptive parents were willing to assume permanent responsibility for children who were not healthy white infants. More resistant were those agencies and social workers committed to infant adoptions who found the added effort and the risks associated with what were called special needs placements, less attractive for either personal or professional reasons. But even they were won over to the new direction in adoption services as it became clear that changing social morés and the legalization of abortion were reducing the number of healthy white infants available for adoption.

Private agencies and 'marketing' services that advertised the availability of adoptable children[2] were also organized by advocates to focus solely on placing children who would otherwise remain in foster or institutional care until they reached legal majority. The successes boasted by these new organizations encouraged the more resistant adoption services to enter into the special needs arena. However, special needs adoption was not without its critics among child welfare advocates, particularly those who saw foster care and adoption as only another example of the victimization of poor, powerless families, particularly single parent families headed by women who were, and still remain, the most vulnerable to the vicissitudes of poverty.

For these advocates, adoption was a remedial act, and a poor one at that, for the victims of a social system that offered little in the way of substantive help to troubled families in averting the crises that led to foster care. They reasoned the obvious: that if social agencies were to emphasize preventive services, the need for child placements would be substantially diminished, and that if agency resources were re-deployed to the front end of the system, fewer resources would be needed at the back end for maintaining children in out-of-home care. This theory of preventive services led some to emphasize permanency planning, largely a case management tool, and others to focus on family centered practice based on the idea that doing so would alleviate most of the need for either permanency planning or adoption.

Oregon's Children's Services Department professionals developed the permanency planning program after winning a grant with a simple imperative from the Children's Bureau: each child should have a family of her own, the birth family if return to her birth parents was a desirable outcome, or through adoption, if it was not. When the program was adopted as an initiative by the Children's Bureau, the number of children in foster care, nationally, was over 500,000. By 1982, the number had decreased to 262,000. Permanency planning took a long view of services to children by creating definable decision points for child welfare cases along a continuum: planning for prevention of placement, reunification after placement, and termination of parental rights and adoption when reunification was unfeasible.

Although initial evaluation results appeared to be positive, the problems that public child welfare faced were overwhelming—money and staff uppermost among them. The lack of resources reduces the agency's capacity to plan or to provide the services that would make 'permanency' possible, and the foster care census began to climb once again (Schorr 2000, 5). Permanency planning was compatible with the third initiative, in-home family-based services, the utility of which was being demonstrated in isolated agencies around the country. The first of these on record, the St. Paul Family Centered Project that operated from 1948 to 1968, had ceased to exist at the time the permanency planning initiative was begun. However, other agencies were adopting family therapy techniques in the 1960s and early 1970s, and were prepared to provide the preventive services that the permanency planning initiative prescribed.

Permanency planning was, and remains, a case management tool for agencies that are legally responsible for children in foster care. Family based service was developed largely in the private sector. Although complementary initiatives, policy makers were slow to recognize their compatibility. Permanency planning was written into federal child welfare policy in 1980 with the Adoption Assistance and Child Welfare Act (Public Law 96-272); however, it took another seventeen years before the Adoption and Safe Families Act of 1997 acknowledged family preservation services. Federal funding that was designated for 'non-categorical' social services was substantially reduced in the early 1980s. Without funds permanency planning became a hollow promise.

Few practitioners in child welfare are opposed absolutely to the use of foster care for abused and neglected children. Foster care may be the only alternative for a family that is so dysfunctional that it is beyond helping within a time frame that respects a child's needs for care and nurture. As Wald (1988) states in an article questioning the wisdom of adopting family based practice without supporting data:

> Although many studies accurately describe the problems involving the foster care system, none provide an answer to these key questions: Is it better to leave a child who has been abused or neglected at home? Is a good foster home worse than a bad home? Foster care may have its problems, but we must remember that the alternative may be worse (36).

These are good questions and the answer to them is, It depends. It depends on whether the family's worker has the time, diagnostic and treatment skills, and resources to work closely with family members to prevent further abuse or neglect. If these are present, the odds are that a child who is not in a home that can be made safe, will be removed. In the same article, Wald describes the improvement in education and emotional well-being of the forty foster children in his study compared with forty children who remained with their parents. However, the sample was not randomly selected and is too small to be generalizable. Without knowing the reasons for their removal, we must ask whether the same results could not have been realized for the children in the placement group had family therapy been made available to their families.

## The Relationship of Family Therapy to Social Work and Child Welfare

In the Gomberg memorial conference papers Weston La Barre (1960, 8-9) describes the family as the fundamental human institution, and the family caseworker's role as fundamental in helping this institution become more usefully and healthily adaptive. He describes the nature of human nature as that of a family-living animal. La Barre, an ethnographer, underscores the importance of the institution of the family even for those families that would seem atypical and dysfunctional. The term dysfunctional is contestable, since many would agree that such behaviors exist in all families, most never experiencing intervention by mental health or social work professionals. The history of other families is characterized by a series of professional interventions.

The family as the object of professional intervention has varied from time to time depending largely on the theory-at-hand. For example, Guerin and Chabot (1992) trace cycles in the history of psychotherapy: "When emotional problems were viewed as a by-product of neurological or moral failings the individual's family was seen as victimized by the dysfunctional member. As psychological theories moved toward explanations based on experiences in nurturing, families came to be viewed as the malignant victimizer (225)." More recently, the family as a unit is seen by therapists in the family therapy movement as neither victim nor victimizer, but as client. A revival of the nature-nurture dichotomy (Guerin and Chabot 1992) has occurred as advances in biological psychiatry and neuropsychology identify genetic sources as origins of behaviors.

The conflict for social work as a discipline seems to have been a dissonance between the traditional social-community focus and the medical-psychological focus, and the inability to integrate the two. Sanford Sherman (1960) describes the chronology of social casework as originating with a primarily social and sociological approach to individual and family problems. However, in an effort to understand the discrepancies between objective facts and subjective experiences, social workers turned to psychological, then psychiatric, then psychoanalytic concepts that resulted in a social work model of personality that was bio-psychic in character. "In casework thinking, inner and outer stresses were clearly separated (Sherman 1960, 15)." However, by the early 1940s, the inadequacies of this model were beginning to be questioned in the social work literature, although it would take several more decades before the family as a focus of theory and treatment became common. Sherman observed:

> In theory, caseworkers affirm the importance of social and cultural influences on the client's personality and his problem; but in practice they find it difficult to use their knowledge of these influences, except peripherally. In characteristic fashion, caseworkers have taken one of two opposing courses in trying to resolve this dilemma. Either they look upon other than emotional factors as incidental and ancillary, or they suggest— especially with reference to the socially disorganized and depressed or "hard-core" family—that a kind of social therapy be attempted without reference to clinical skills (16).

The introduction of family therapy (although it was not so called) to the field of social work has been attributed to the functionalist school whose major contributors were Virginia Robinson, Jesse Taft, and Rosa Wessel of the University of Pennsylvania School of Social Work (Hartman and Laird 1983, 18), and to the work of various Jewish family service agencies staffed by University of Pennsylvania graduates. Perhaps most influential on the field of child and family social work was the family casework of the Jewish Family Service agency of New York and the Family Mental Health Clinic, established in 1956, and supervised by psychiatrist, Nathan Ackerman. Although Ackerman's name is not well known today, his early work in family diagnosis and treatment and his association with social workers at the Jewish Family Service agency are attributed to the early development of family-focused treatment in the social work profession.

Robert Gomberg, also an important figure in the development of family casework, was the director of Jewish Family Service of New York from 1949 until his early death in 1958. As a tribute to Gomberg, an interdisciplinary conference was held in 1960. It culminated in the publication of a collection of papers on the theoretical and practical developments in family diagnosis, treatment, and research by theorists and practitioners representing social work, psychiatry and the social sciences (Ackerman, Beatman and Sherman 1960). This formal recognition of the family unit as the focus of therapy was mainly limited to middle class clients who were able to pay for services, and who sought help for their problems, unlike the captive families that became the focus of family centered programs a decade later.

Hartman and Laird (1983) suggest that social workers who embraced family casework tended to become family therapists; their work was published in family therapy, not in social work journals. The field of social work continued to vacillate between an emphasis on the individual or diagnostic school representing the inner focus, and the social order or functionalist school representing the outer focus, as the primary source of social problems and as the target for change (Hartman and Laird, 19). The authors explain that:

> This dichotomous view of person and situation may well have had implications for the place of the family in social work practice theory. Sometimes it almost seemed that the family, like a child in a 'no-win' position between battling parents, got caught between social work's two competing, sometimes warring, approaches. To those concerned with social change, the family focus was 'too psychological,' whereas, for those exploring the psychology of the individual, the family was lost as a result of the 'inner' focus (20).

This ambivalence by social workers over their roles in relation to the individual and society may have been at issue; however, there was also the field's obsession with professionalism, historically equated in psychotherapeutic work with the individual, and more recently, with the individual in private practice. Contributors to the nascent family therapy movement, on the other hand, were revolting against Freudian psychotherapy. Not unlike the 'rank-and-file' movement that occurred with the advent of the New Deal, the proliferation of new social programs in the early 1930s, and the influx of 'paraprofessionals' and non-professionals in the Great Society social programs of the 1960s, family-centered practitioners in the early 1970s included therapists without social work training. The notion of empowering families, an extension of the activist-clients of the 1960s welfare rights movement, was viewed by many in social work as an encroachment on their professionalism and their professional prerogatives.

## *The Role of Administration in Social Work and Child Welfare*

In describing the child welfare system in Chapter 1, we suggested that barriers to the adoption of family centered practice, particularly in the public child welfare agency, are due in part to the traditional, bureaucratized organizational structure of social agencies and the inhibiting effect that this structure has on an agency's ability to accept and effect change. This structure, according to Wilensky and Lebeaux

(1958, 231) has its antecedents in the proliferation of New Deal programs in the 1930s and the growth in the number of social agencies required to administer them. The bureaucratic organization was firmly entrenched by this time.

Classical management theorists, like Henri Fayol, F. W. Mooney, and Lyndall Urwick had developed the principles that are recognized in the organizational chart: "a pattern of precisely defined jobs organized in a hierarchical manner through precisely defined lines of command and communication (Morgan 1986, 29)." Skocpol (1995) argues that bureaucratization and professionalization in government originated in the states at the local level, spreading to the federal government only after the New Deal and only after passing through state legislatures. Descriptions by Mangold (1934) of the development of county welfare departments supports Skocpol's claim.

The mechanistic, or machine-like organization was designed to mass produce materials and products, and to fight wars efficiently. Its extension into the domain of social services was a natural enough response to the dilemma of rapidly increasing services. However, the recipients of services are neither materials nor products, and the war being waged is economic not military. Sociologist, Max Weber (1958), seems resigned to the inevitability of bureaucracy, likening it to an iron cage:

> The Puritan wanted to work in a calling; we are forced to do so. For when asceticism was carried out of monastic cells into everyday life, and began to dominate worldly morality, it did its part in building the tremendous cosmos of the modern economic order. This order is now bound to the technical and economic conditions of machine production which to-day determine the lives of all the individuals who are born into this mechanism, not only those directly concerned with economic acquisition, with irresistible force. Perhaps it will so determine them until the last ton of fossilized coal is burnt. In Baxter's view the care for external goods should only rest on the shoulders of the 'saint like a light cloak, which can be thrown aside at any moment'. But fate decreed that the cloak should become an iron cage (181).

In their description of bureaucracy in the social agency, Wilensky and Lebeaux portray a classical pyramidal design with a formalized rule structure and centralized control to achieve maximum efficiency, a career ladder, and a supervisory pattern that the authors characterize as specifically social work-like in orientation.[3] They describe a supervisor-trainee model, still in use in social work, which is not unlike the doctor-resident relationship in medicine. Unlike the doctor-resident relationship which ceases once the training regimen has concluded, the supervisor-worker relationship used in the public social service agency continues even after the caseworker becomes experienced and skilled in her job (Wilensky and Lebeaux 1958, 239).

At the time Wilensky and Lebeaux were writing, the social work model of supervision was seen as an impediment to professional acceptance; however, contrary to their prediction that the supervisory model would erode, the growth of social programs that occurred in the 1960s with the influx of workers without formal training reinforced the model. The authors describe the relationship of the bureaucratic agency as one of obstacles and impediments, noting that these rules and red tape "reach out to mold the client [who is called on to] behave like a 'case' if he is to use the service (240)." This includes waiting for lengthy periods of time, completing forms, following the rules, and, one might safely conclude, figuring out how to circumvent them.

Theologian Paul Tillich wrote in 1961, that the most important representative of social work is the caseworker, who must respond sensitively and spontaneously to the needs of the client; however, the caseworker must guard against the temptation to transform care into control. "He is in danger of imposing instead of listening, and acting mechanically instead of reacting spontaneously. Every social worker knows this danger, but not always does he notice that he himself may have already fallen to this temptation." Tillich offers the example of the ubiquitous 'case', a word that makes the person into something general: ". . . [it] makes him into an object for whom everything is determined and in whom spontaneity is suppressed (14)." The human relations skills that were developing in non-social work disciplines were, oddly, eluding social work administration, despite the skills required for understanding human behavior in social casework (Simmons 1961). The language of administration is rife with such examples: can one be a caseworker without referring to cases?

Although current child welfare administrators may have softened their approaches to managing their employees and their relationships with their peers in the community in keeping with current trends in personnel practices, the bureaucratic agency and its hierarchical structure remain a fixture in state and local agencies. Nevertheless, it has been difficult to reconcile the need for structure in administering child welfare agencies with the need for flexibility in working with disorganized families. Perhaps this paradox is in part what motivates social workers to enter into private practice where freedom from command-and-control structures affords them the flexibility to work creatively with their clients.

## Early Family Centered Practices

In the complex social welfare system that evolved during the twentieth century, it is difficult to pinpoint 'firsts'. However, it appears from our review of the literature that the private sector is generally the innovator, a circumstance attributable largely to a greater flexibility for action. Government organizations, local, state and federal, are necessarily slower to embrace change, and tend to field new practices only after evidence is apparent that some form of policy response is desirable. This has clearly been the case with family centered practice the origins of which are generally attributed to the work of a group of consultants, administrators and practitioners who developed the St. Paul Family Centered Project in Ramsey County, St. Paul, Minnesota. The project began in 1948, and ended twenty years later in 1968.

The St. Paul project attempted to integrate 108 public and private agency services that dealt with four major human problems specific to dependency, ill-health, maladjustment, and recreational needs found in families whose children were known at the time to the juvenile justice system. Bradley Buell was the Executive Director of Community Research Associates, a New York consulting firm, and one of the principals in the development of the St. Paul project research study. With an eerily contemporary ring to it, Buell, writing about the project in 1952, describes rather dramatically the core importance of community to Americans. He warns that, "The vital spirit of America's protest against the inevitability of human ills is in danger of becoming lost among protests against irrationalities in its organized expression (Buell 1952, 5)." He further cautions that the complexities of the organized system obscure the real issues that the much derided formal social welfare system grew up around. Implying that human needs are at the heart of the problem, Buell reminds the reader that ". . . family strengths and weaknesses constitute powerful assets and liabilities in the treatment and cure of many different kinds of problems. But strangely enough [professionals] sometimes forget or overlook the family in preoccupation with a part of its problem . . . (9)."

The study design attempted to measure the complex set of circumstances present in the St. Paul service community and Buell was thoroughly criticized for it. In his view, counting contacts with agencies could be construed as a reliable means for determining the degree of 'maladjustment' exhibited by a particular family: the greater the number of contacts, the greater their maladjustment. However, Buell's system was criticized as overly simplistic. Lukoff and Mencher (1962, 437) pointed out the circularity inherent in arguments based on quantifying families by the number of problems or prevalence rates in the use of community services. If the number of problem families is contingent on the number and variety of services available in the community, then communities with few or no services should have no problem families.

Buell and his organization were influential consultants in many of the country's communities over several decades. Their work points to the influence that a few 'experts' can have on local service organizations desperate for answers to many of the social problems that beset their communities. Although Buell's prescriptions have been largely discredited, and the St. Paul project ended after twenty years, the project provides a context for understanding later efforts to implement family based practices.

## The St. Paul Family-Centered Project

Beulah Compton, a professor at the University of Minnesota School of Social Work whose involvement in the project spanned eighteen years, writes that the St. Paul Project was divided into three phases. The first phase was the Family Unit Reporting Study (1948-1952); the second was the Family Centered Project Treatment and Research Effort (1952-1959); and, the third was the Work Reorientation Project (1960-1968). During the first phase, the Family Unit Reporting Study reviewed 55,000 cases. According to Compton, 40 percent of the community's families used public and private social services during the month of November, about 6 percent of whom suffered from problems that were serious enough to absorb over half of the combined services of the agencies reviewed.

The focus of the Community Research team's research was "the prevention and control of human pathology. . . through the early identification and coordinated treatment of the family unit (Compton 1979, 2)." By counting the number of official disorders found in a family, defined as official contacts with community agencies, it was proposed that family problems could be approached in an organized and coordinated manner and that a community plan for the prevention of family disorganization could be developed. The second phase (1952-1959) was the Family Centered Project Treatment and Research Effort.

Half of the project families came from the 1948 study, and the other half from the Ramsey County Welfare Department's Division of Protective Services. Conditions for family involvement included the presence of a child under eighteen who was in danger of delinquency or verifiable neglect, the presence of family health or financial problems, and the presence of problems that, in the view of the screeners, rendered them unreachable by active community agencies. Initial treatment and research began with an attempt at the early identification of multi-problem families, described by Compton as case finding. The idea was to locate these families early, provide them with services, and prevent or forestall further deterioration.

Compton traced the patterns of family contacts with agencies and discovered that most of those interviewed were already known to agencies "for long, long years (3)." It turned out that adequacy of services was a greater problem than early identification of families. Compton's report recommended that more emphasis be placed on helping families when they first appeared at an agency, and that more concern be given to the manner in which professionals relate to families in trouble. However, her report was not published by the project, she suspects, because it was an indictment of participating agencies (5). The project did adopt the position that 'case finding' was futile unless the agencies provided services, a position that led to the development in 1954, of working agreements among seven community agencies to participate in the Family Centered Project.

Under the terms of the agreement, these agencies would lend workers to the project, each carrying a caseload of twenty project families. Workers, were paid and managed administratively by their home agencies, were supervised by the project, and attended project training seminars at which participants were encouraged to experiment with different casework and treatment modalities. They were encouraged to share their experiences with one another in a supportive, collegial environment. Similar seminars were organized for supervisors at which they were encouraged to share common problems including gaps in services and issues that grew out of their inter-agency relationships. Agency executives and community leaders participated in similar groups, each focusing on the administration and coordination of the project and its participants.

As Compton notes, ". . . the Family Centered project involved a great deal more than the development of casework method. Its basic foundation was in community organization (5)." Ludwig Geismar and Beverly Ayres, who were contracted to conduct a study of the Family Centered project, reviewed 150 closed cases and found that 65.3 percent showed evidence of a positive change, 18.7 percent showed no change, and 16 percent changed for the worse. Typically, families evidenced small gains, with those with fewer problems at the onset showing a moderate change, and those with more problems at the onset, showing considerable gains, or a failure to change.

By the time the treatment phase of the project ended in June 1959, the project staff had identified five principles for a successful community-based family-centered program: 1) reaching out to families who are unable to ask for help; 2) a total family approach; 3) collaboration with the family and among agencies; 4) identifying and marshaling the strengths of family members; and, 5) placing the responsibility for coordinating all aspects of service planning and treatment with one worker. The methods used by the project's practitioners in operationalizing these principles were published by the project in the Casework Notebook in 1959.[4] Compton reports that relations were contentious among the project's professional caseworkers and the Community Research Services consultants over the direction of the project.

The treatment staff resisted the idea that identifying families and coordinating services would result in better services to people, seeing in this effort a movement toward social control of families and community control of agencies. There was disagreement over Buell's notion that these families could be identified by 'official contacts' with certain community agencies and institutions, and that such contacts indicated *prima facie* evidence of 'pathology'. There was also violent disagreement over Community Research Associates' idea that all efforts at help should be directed to the families with the least 'pathology' under the assumption that help to them was more efficient over the long haul of a family's life (6).

The differences that emerged were, no doubt, more complex than the simple classification into administrative and treatment decisions. The desire of Buell and his associates to create a model for identifying and counting families along the lines of their earlier efforts to systematize diagnosis and case finding using empirical evidence, was probably attributable to a broader objective. Buell and his consultants were creating a generic model that was transferable across communities, while the treatment objectives of local project caseworkers hinged on their credibility and integrity in the use of professional judgment and practice skills—another example of clashing discourses.

The third phase of the project began in 1960, and extended through the end of the project in 1968. The goals of the Work Orientation Program phase, were: 1) to formulate and execute a comprehensive orientation and training program to expand family-centered treatment and intensive training for the Ramsey County Welfare Department staff in the use of the Work Reorientation Project procedures; 2) to assist Ramsey County Welfare Department with becoming a family-centered casework agency by late 1961; and, 3) to organize other public and private agencies to follow the Ramsey County Department's lead by implementing family-centered treatment along the lines of the Work Reorientation Project guidelines.

Compton claims that this last goal created dissension among many of the community's professional leaders. It called for developing a community reporting system based on a family unit count with the purpose of providing up-to-date information on the types of problems families exhibited. It also called for mapping service trends and proposed the use of the family centered caseworkers as instructors in the Work Reorientation seminars, all of which were seen as an infringement on the individual agency's prerogatives. Agency workers were being asked to complete a 16-page schedule that they felt was an imposition on their time and irrelevant to their work with families. Project staff and researchers questioned the Community Research Associates' definition of pathology, and objected to the idea that the focus of the agencies' efforts should be on less troubled families who were more likely to succeed. The researcher's desire for empiricism was at cross-purposes with the caseworker's more immediate concerns for working with troubled families. Then, as now, two worthy objectives cancel each other out, leaving the field with little but the exhortations of workers who have only anecdotal evidence to support their need for more resources.

The problems that the St. Paul Family-Centered project experienced appear, in hindsight, minor relative to its successes. It is possible that the last phase of the project, in which the agency leadership grew at odds with the Community Research Associates consultants, defeated the good work of the previous family treatment phase. The researchers also complained that the project's publications, which were published locally, were not widely disseminated. And, of course, as is often the case when the principals in a project of this magnitude quarrel, problems associated with the project overshadow its positive features, leaving acrimony, defensiveness, and no one to speak in its favor.

The controversy over the wisdom of a pathology-based system for identifying families went beyond the St. Paul Family-Centered project to the field of social work, generally. As Geismar (1971) indicates in the introduction to his book, *Family and Community Functioning*:

> The reciprocal relationship between family and community is well illustrated in the controversy that raged during the mid-sixties over the use of the concept multi-problem family. Responding to a flood of speeches and articles describing the characteristics of the multi-problem family, a number of writers, concerned with the function of the welfare system, pointed to its serious shortcomings and the reciprocal relationship between family and community problems. They believed, in effect, that the term multi-problem agency or community better characterized the problem situation than the concept multi-problem family (7).

The St. Paul project's focus on the family was adopted by a small but growing group of mental health professionals and social workers seeking a treatment shift from the 'individual to the family' and the 'individual *and* family' to the 'individual *in* family' (Hartman and Laird 1983). References to the St. Paul Family Centered Project began appearing in the family preservation literature in the late 1970s.

## The Spread of Family-Based Services

Typical of the programs designed to treat individuals in the context of their families were those developed in several Midwestern states in the late 1960s and early 1970s. These programs claimed that intensive (concerted) efforts (including family therapy) to help families through difficult periods in their lives were enough to keep most families intact, to prevent their long-term involvement with social services, and the continuing downward trend of dysfunctional behaviors that culminates with family dissolution.

Acting on the assumption that many of the families involved with social services agencies lack basic home management and child-rearing skills, the proponents of in-home, family-based services believed that such skills could be learned, much as children learn from watching their parents, from an experienced professional who was able to model appropriate behaviors while transcending the organizational barriers associated with conventional social service programs. Workers went into families' homes, rather than requiring that families come to the agency and were given license to spend as much time as was needed to work with families on their own turf. Caseloads were small; workers were trained and enjoyed a collegial relationship that encouraged sharing problems and insights for their solution.

Depending on their particular service philosophy, these agencies employed people with a range of skills and professional expertise from master's degree social workers and psychologists, to individuals with other degrees in the social sciences. Some were staffed by trained therapists using variants of behavioral or family systems therapy models. Some programs were free standing; others were part of larger social services and mental health organizations. A few programs operated literally out of employees' automobiles, meeting in limited office space to discuss their day's work. They had in common their commitment to working with family members in their own homes, or in neutral settings not recognizably associated with the official social service apparatus.

Families were referred to these programs by public social service agencies. Fees for services were paid through both formal and informal contracting arrangements with agencies and courts, some operated with foundation grants. For all of these programs, financial stability was tenuous and dependent upon the uncertain political winds that affect most social service agencies. In exchange for this uncertainty, privately operated in-home, family-based organizations enjoyed a flexibility that could not be found in public agencies which were bound up by old habits, bureaucratic inflexibility, limited funds, high worker turnover, and regulatory constraints.

## Conclusion

The context of child welfare today differs from its origins in the charity movement in the late 1800s and early 1900s, in several significant ways. It was, and remains, a program motivated by middle class moral and social values; however, where it once focused on children who were abandoned and destitute, its focus on poverty has been replaced by an emphasis on child abuse and neglect. This is not to say that child abuse and neglect were not recognized among child savers in the late nineteenth and early twentieth centuries—the Society for the Prevention of Cruelty to Children was begun in 1874 in response to a child's abuse in foster care. However, it did not materialize as a community problem that required public policy intervention until the mid-1960s.

Despite periodic federal initiatives designed to remedy the failings of the child welfare system, few seem to become more than window dressing. The system is still tethered to the bureaucratic and administrative rule structures that were designed to promote efficiency and were adopted by social worker administrators in the 1930s. The discourses of social work that developed around the commitment to children and families in need are attenuated by the discourses of bureaucracy and administration. As we will see in the coming chapters, bureaucratic discourses are inadequate to the helping task.

The efficiency paradigm (Lubove 1965) has not been tempered by the obvious: services to disorganized families and bureaucratic efficiencies are a poor fit. The tools and techniques acquired by family therapists in their work with private clients are, its proponents suggest, equally useful with the clients of public child welfare agencies. However, rule-bound organizations militate against the flexibility that these tools and techniques require. At the same time, the field of public administration has largely ignored the social agencies that have the welfare of children and families as their mission. It may be that the multiple discourses operating in the child welfare arena create 'blank noise',[5] where everyone is talking at once, and no one is listening.

---

## Notes

[1] Over 500,00 children were in foster care in the 1970s. Permanency planning initiatives are credited with reducing this number by at least one-third; however, the number has climbed to over half a million children in 1999.

[2] These organizations advertised children, often nationally, to adoptive parents and adoption agencies using photographs and biographical sketches written to encourage interest in so-called waiting children. Other creative methods were used to the same purpose.

[3] See also, Street, Elwood (1931). *Social Work Administration*. New York: Harper & Brothers, on a 'handbook' of administration for the private social agency, which, in quoting from Mary Parker Follett's "Some discrepancies in Leadership, Theory and Practice", notes the importance of prefacing orders with 'please'.

[4] A second edition of the Casework Notebook was prepared by Alice Overton and Katherine H. Tinker, and published by the Greater St. Paul Community Chest and Councils, Inc., in 1970.

[5] Salvador Minuchin, personal interview, October 7, 1999. Boston, MA.

# Chapter 3

## The Orphaning of Child Welfare

"If a child is to be heard, he must be killed"[1]

### Introduction

Child psychiatrist and family therapist, Salvador Minuchin exhorts mental health experts to examine their tendencies to operationalize social problems in doable segments while disclaiming responsibility for their larger effects using the example of la turret. The story is as follows:

> From earliest times, infants were abandoned by their parents. In France in the early eighteenth century, unwanted newborns were often left on the porches of churches, private residences, and convents. Many died before they were found, most died soon after. Concerned experts operationalized the problem, reducing it to manageable terms in this way: Unwed mothers were abandoning their infants in order to save their families' honor. If a way could be found to preserve the anonymity of these mothers perhaps the babies could be saved. Technology provided an ingenious solution. A turntable was installed in the door of the foundling hospital. A baby could be placed on the turntable (*la turret*) and passed through an opening in the door into the institution. It was not necessary to open the door, so no one saw

the donor. Family honor could be saved and so could the child. The results of this humane policy staggered the authorities. The order of St. Vincent DePaul, which sheltered 312 children when *la turret* was established, in 1740 had 3,150. In 1784, there were 40,000 and in 1833, 131,000. Children were out-placed with foster families and wet nurses who were paid for their services. It wasn't long before the anonymous parents were abandoning their infants only to be paid as their caretakers. What was at that time in history thought to be a well-meaning policy was not, and the doors of the foundling hospitals eventually resumed their unbroken shape (Minuchin and Elizur 1990, 26).[2][3]

In child welfare, operationalizing segments of a problem (and running the risk of finding solutions for the wrong problem) is not an uncommon response when family problems seem limitless and the system is overwhelmed with clients. Using his considerable expertise in family therapy, Minuchin worked with the families of children in New York City's foster care population, learning first hand the considerable frustrations that organized child welfare creates for its official helpers and its clients, alike. He used his superior expertise to demonstrate that family therapy techniques were appropriate for public child welfare clients and could achieve unimagined results.

## Multiple Discourses in Child Welfare

We have suggested that there are multiple discourses operating in the public child welfare system and that the presence of these discourses, with their divergent and conflicting ideologies and languages, create a confusion of meanings that stymie the liberating process of change. In this chapter, we argue that these conflicting discourses have led to the orphaning of child welfare, and the creation of a new child welfare discourse that is epistemologically uni-dimensional and lacking in the dialectical attributes that would give it shape and meaning as a discipline. Discourse theory offers the possibility of a crosscutting analysis that transcends disciplinary rhetoric and ideology. In this case, each of the three discourses we discuss in the context of the child welfare system (social work, family therapy, and public administration) affects the others in some observable manner. Furthermore, by acknowledging the relevance of these discourses to child welfare, responsibility for the functions of child welfare, from helpful to harmful, can be more usefully addressed.

Discourse refers to the language and meanings that constitute the ideologies of these disciplines. Social work theorist, David Howe (1994) writes that the ". . . formation of a particular discourse creates contingent centers of power which define areas of knowledge, passing truths and frameworks of explanation and understanding. Those with power can control the language of discourse and can therefore influence how the world is to be seen and what it shall mean (522)." Power in child welfare is singularly one-sided with control in the hands of a power structure that is, itself, in disarray. The result is that those clients who become caught up in the web-like child welfare system are subject to life-influencing decisions that are sometimes arbitrary and at the very least, frustrating. (Two families in similar circumstances may experience very different outcomes, depending solely on the competence and resources of their caseworkers.) The ease with which policy makers alter the balance in power between competing interests in the complex matter of ministering to the needs of families points to a simplistic understanding about the relationships between structures and discourse at both micro and macro levels. Here we use micro to refer to the family itself, and the officials (caseworkers) who interact with family members, and macro to refer to the larger system that includes child welfare structures as well as the policies—both economic and social--that too often create the circumstances that lead to family dysfunction.

Through discourse analysis, ideologies and determinants of behavior are deconstructed while guarding against the trap of false consciousness (in supposing that there must be true consciousness) and while attempting to avoid simplistic claims about relationships between structures and discourse (Farmer 1999 4). The challenge is to examine discourses and structures without resorting to some grand design, as exemplified in the history of organized child welfare, where, through repeated claims of grand solutions to the complex and interrelated problems of families, its repeated failures become evident. The fields of social work, family therapy (often described in a disciplinary context as marriage and family therapy), and public administration differ from one another ideologically, and in the meanings given to both subject and language and yet each has been influential, by degree, in the construction of child welfare practices and policies.

Social work's ideological origins in the matter of child welfare are in child saving; public administration's ideological origins are in bureaucratic efficiency; and family therapy's ideological contribution to child welfare is in extending the therapeutic boundaries from the voluntary to the involuntary family. Social work and public administration are inextricably entwined in the matter of social welfare as is made obvious by Mangold (1934) and Browning (1948), discussed below. For example, in the field of social work, the language of child welfare remains in the realm of child saving as it has since it united reformers from disparate causes following the economic depression of 1893. Child saving became a rallying point when economic depression exposed the devastating circumstances of impoverished children and the failures of public and private relief efforts of the earlier period following reconstruction (Katz 1996, 117). Children were saved from oppressive child labor laws and abject poverty, from delinquency, and from neglecting and abusing parents. The subsequent proliferation of charitable programs, both public and private, led to the intervention of the state as administrator, supervisor, and later, as surrogate parent.

In response to out-of-home placement of children, the Children's Committee of the National Conference of Social Work (1906) and the White House Conference of 1909 emphasized the importance of home life for children, prompting a move to give public pensions to mothers with dependent children. During this period, the responsibility for children and mothers' pensions remained with local welfare boards, or their equivalent, or with the court that handled juvenile cases.[4] However, as counties found it more difficult to afford relief for the poor, and as discrepancies in the treatment, or lack of treatment of certain populations of needy and handicapped persons became evident, county responsibilities gave way to state administration and supervision. Mangold, writing in 1934, opens a window on the bureaucratization of social services when he observes that a greatly expanded public welfare necessitated "greater uniformity among the counties and cities in respect to methods, standards, disposition of cases, cost of work, and to other items in a philanthropic program [which] forced the states to inspect, recommend, and in some cases supervise the work of the local public welfare body (36)."

Despite the growth of public welfare bureaucracies in the United States, the attention given by social work professionals to administering these programs in the social work literature of the period is sparse. An article written by Browning in 1948, in the *Social Service Review* suggests that knowledge gained from the new field of public administration to the specialized field of public welfare would be helpful (Browning, 1948). She makes the case for strong, competent administrators in public welfare agencies, who are attuned to the needs of their service recipients, willing to learn from their social worker staff, and capable of planning and statesmanship[5] in operating welfare services, both large and small. Browning states:

> There is, of course, no area of public administration which does not in some way touch on human welfare. Whether applied to engineering, medicine, finance, or social work services in government, public administration must serve the best interests of individual citizens if the aims of the community are to be attained. It is a common observation that unpaved and uncared-for alleys and streets are more likely to be found in the sections of a city where people in low-income groups live. The oldest and most neglected public schools are frequently in those same neighborhoods; and where yards are smallest and children most numerous one may find the least public park space. This is not always true, of course; but it does often happen that the largest amount of tax money is returned in public service to the districts of a city where it came from and where persons of greater influence and prestige make their homes. The point that is important here is that, almost without exception, the recipients of public welfare services are persons of little influence and possessing little of that prestige which is based on economic status. Hence there derives an inescapable responsibility for citizens and particularly for the profession of social work to safeguard the interests of these recipients (10).

Although the field of social work has generally accepted the responsibility for safeguarding the interests of vulnerable citizens, this has not been a common theme in public administration. Their respective discourses appear to have prevented a joint exploration of common ground. Permeability of disciplinary boundaries also plays a role. And, we suspect, issues of permeability, particularly in the social work discipline, have contributed significantly to the orphaning of child welfare.

Public administrators share an eclecticism in backgrounds and training, generally admitting to the profession any professional who works in the public sector. Public administration discourses are multiple, drawing on political science, sociology, business administration, economics, and psychology among others for theoretical and practice insights. Social work, on the other hand, appears fiercely territorial, even tribal in insisting that the boundaries of the profession not be breached. Nevertheless, the theoretical discourses of social work draw freely from medicine, particularly psychiatry, sociology, the administrative sciences, and more recently, family therapy. Family therapy, a much newer, albeit tentative, entrant on the child welfare scene, includes among its most significant contributors anthropologists, psychiatrists, psychologists, social workers, biologists, and cyberneticians.

Early concepts and techniques in family therapy were influenced by cultural anthropologists. They offered alternative perspectives for viewing behavior and pathology by examining the patterns of interactions among family members. Cybernetics has also contributed to the languages of family therapy and public and business administration with terms such as homeostasis, feedback loops, self-correcting systems, and the term system, itself (Bassi 1991, 77). Social work discourse contributed core practice principles to the child welfare system, while public administration contributed the administrative and regulatory structure. Family therapy's contribution is a new language of the therapeutic that builds on psychoanalysis and the varied disciplines of its early contributors. As important, family therapy has opened to question certain core principles of social work practice in child welfare.

## *Family Therapy Discourses.*

As we noted in Chapter 1, two distinctly different therapeutic discourses are associated with family-centered practice in child welfare. One is represented in the family systems approach and its ecological perspective on the structure of families' and members' interactions with one another, and the other is social learning theory which is associated with the behaviorists' educative methods of behavioral change. Both are central to understanding the policies that have evolved around family centered practice. Pioneers in both the family therapy and the behaviorist movements branched out in their respective pursuits in reaction to the limitations of Freudian psychoanalysis, and both were pioneered principally by psychiatrists and psychologists following World War II (Burlingame 1982; Bassi 1991; Glass and Arnkoff, 1995).

Guerin and Chabot (1995) suggest that there were four key groups of theorists that feature prominently in the origins of the family therapy movement, as distinguished from the behaviorists. The communica-tions theory group began in the middle 1950s in The Mental Research Institute at Palo Alto (California) with the work of Gregory Bateson, an anthropologist interested in animal behavior, evolution, ecology, and cybernetics. Bateson, the husband of anthropologist, Margaret Mead, was interested principally in theory building and the science of communication, and drew on Whitehead and Russell's theory of logical types (1910) for his communications model. His interests were in patterns, or systems of communication among family members, not in therapeutic interventions. Significant contributors from the Palo Alto Group included Donald Jackson, Jay Haley, and Virginia Satir. Jeanne Giovannoni[6], who worked with Satir at Palo Alto, describes her as perhaps the most influential of these individuals in spreading family therapy to the field of social work, particularly on the west coast.

Also at about this time, Lyman Winn, another anthropologist, and Murray Bowen, a psychoanalyst, were developing theories of multigenerational systems at the National Institute of Mental Health (NIMH). The multigenerationalists began by studying hospitalized schizophrenic patients and by bringing family members into the hospital for therapies, then moved on to work with less dysfunctional populations. A third group is described as experiential systems theorists who are represented by the work of child psychiatrist, Carl Whitaker and Esalen-trained social worker, Virginia Satir, one of the first teachers of family therapies. Although they worked independently of one another and drew from differing epistemologies for their therapies, they shared much in common in their clinical work which emphasized "intuition, feelings, unconscious processes, and an atheoretical stance (249)."

Yet another group, represented by the structural theorists, emanates from the child guidance movement. Among the significant contributors to this movement were child psychoanalysts, Nathan Ackerman, and Salvadore Minuchin, both of whom were influenced by the work of Harry Stack Sullivan. Ackerman, a neo-Freudian from Columbia, recognized the desirability of bringing families together, rather than dealing with the adults and child individually, as was customary in the psychoanalytic tradition. Minuchin describes many of the early family therapies, including his own work at the time, as treating individuals in family groups.[7] Minuchin's first book, *Families of the Slums* (1967), was a seminal work—first found in libraries in the anthropology listings since family therapy was not then a catalogue designation—describing the work of psychoanalysts, psychologists and social workers at the Wiltwyck School for Boys in New York in the early 1960s. He and his colleagues were among the first to work with poor families and families of color in this NIMH-funded project. At the time the project was begun, the therapeutic experience was white and middle-class; families of the poor were considered to be therapeutically unreachable. They were in uncharted territory with the Wiltwyck families: "Traditional clinical procedures simply would not have been feasible, workable, or justifiable (9)". Their approach explored the structure and dynamics of delinquent-producing, disadvantaged, disorganized families using the techniques and interventions of family therapy, rather than individual psychotherapy. The results of this four year exploratory research project were further developed by Minuchin and his colleagues at the Philadelphia Child Guidance Clinic where Minuchin was clinical director for about ten years, and later directed its family therapy training program for nearly as long. Despite their differences, there was significant interchange among the early family therapy theorists as they moved freely among these groups in their quest for new techniques. The work done by Philadelphia Child Guidance is significant in this discussion, as is the Wiltwyck project, since both centered on under served poor families, most of whom were African- and Hispanic-American.

Some thirty years earlier, the social work profession became embroiled in a struggle that divided the field into two camps: the diagnostic school which sought personality transformation through long-term, in-depth understanding of the client's life history, and the short-term reality-based, functional school which was influenced by the humanistic psychoanalysis of Otto Rank (Ehrenreich 1985, 126). Guided principally by Virginia Robinson and Jesse Taft, faculty at the Pennsylvania University School of Social Work, the functionalists are credited with important contributions to the family therapy movement (Burlingame 1982; Siporin 1980), although functionalism pre-dated developments in family therapy by several decades. (For a critique of this period in social work, see Ehrenreich 1985.)

Also contributing to the therapeutic discourses of family centered practice are the behaviorists who were not originally considered family therapists. B.F. Skinner is credited with introducing behavior therapy in the United States in his 1953 book, *Science and Human Behavior* in which the treatment of psychological problems is described using conditioning principles. Operant contingency management techniques such as behavior modification and applied behavioral analysis were used principally in the treatment of serious psychological disorders of institutionalized patients. These techniques were not taken seriously by the medical profession except as useful tools in the management of aberrant behaviors. The early behaviorists were scorned by their colleagues in psychiatry and psychoanalysis who found their research using institutionalized patients ethically questionable, and by the public whose perceptions of behavioral techniques was formed in part, by Stanley Kubrick's 1971 film, *A Clockwork Orange* (Glass and Arnkoff 1992). However, the ethical concerns of professionals about behaviorists' techniques began to change during the 1970s as the use of behavior management methods gained new adherents. The new behaviorists participated in the organization of several professional associations and the publication of several new research journals.

The contribution of the behaviorists to child welfare practice occurred principally with the early work of Gerald Patterson (1972), whose research using social learning theory to train parents to alter the behavior of aggressive children was influential in the development of several early family centered programs. Social learning theory emphasizes the role of other people as agents of reinforcement, particularly when these others are influential in the patient's life. It focuses on modeling and imitation, meaning that the subject need not reproduce a behavior, but can learn it as effectively by observing and imitating the behavior of another. "Social learning theory departs from behaviorism in that it recognizes cognitive forces as mediating factors between the environment and individual behavior" (Howard and Hollander 1997, 45). The successful use of behavior modification and social learning theory techniques with the parents of institutionalized children led to the creation, by psychologist Donald Stover, of a new program of roving clinicians acting as change agents in the homes and schools of children who would otherwise have been institutionalized (Fahl and Morrisey 1979). This was a promising breakthrough in the placement prevention repertoire; however, the interest it elicited from public child welfare agencies was limited.

A few small contract programs that shared similar therapeutic philosophies, both systems and behaviorist, were begun in the late 1960s and the 1970s. They proliferated into the mid- to late 1980s following a series of grants made by the Children's Bureau, Department of Health and Human Services, and the Edna McConnell Clark Foundation of New York. Elements of family centered practice have since been incorporated into some public child welfare programs; however, these are the exception, not the rule. The structure of child welfare agencies is, in part, responsible for the difficulties these agencies have experienced in adopting family centered practice models; however, competing discourses in the family centered movement itself created contentious relationships among its principal advocates. The two most prevalent discourses are the social learning theorists, commonly associated with family preservation models, and the cybernetics-systems therapists using a structural-ecological approach associated with family-based service models.

Whether the program has as its theoretical framework family systems theory, social learning theory, community systems theory, or some other treatment-casework modality, working with the family as a whole, including siblings, grandparents, and historically ignored fathers, is the common denominator. This kinship focus marks a paradigmatic shift for public child welfare practice since, to accomplish this objective, the people who work with families must be good diagnosticians, good therapists, and good case managers—a tall order, indeed. As we have noted, the programmatic barriers to integrating family centered practice into the community of child and family services have to do with worker willingness and preparedness, and systemic impediments not unlike those found in the families themselves.

Adoption of the family preservation approach was further stymied by its own advocates who squandered much of their political capital by squabbling among themselves and succumbing to over blown claims for the success of their preferred approaches to working with families. Fierce competition among child welfare programs for scarce funding has set natural allies against one another and created contentious environments in which stakeholders attempt to out-do each other with hyperbolic claims of success. Child welfare administrators, who in our experience tend to be conservative managers, prefer to use their own scarce resources on sure bets. In all, the clients are the losers. Child welfare has lost its strongest traditional advocates, professional social workers, schools of social work, and social work's professional organizations[8] to individual therapy and private practice. As the dominant discourse, though, social work militates against incursions into its putative territory by family therapists, and public administrationists whose own ambivalence towards public social welfare overcomes any inclinations to resist dominant pressures. As a result, the child welfare system has been orphaned, ignored by actual and potential stakeholders, policy makers and the public.

## Public Administration and Bureaucratic Discourses

We suggest that the inattentiveness of public administrationists may be reinforced by the social work profession which has insisted that managers and administrators in these agencies be social workers first.

A recent study of cross-disciplinary publications by public administration scholars (Rodgers and Rodgers 2000) shows that less than 1
percent of respondents published in the field of social work although 63
percent published in disciplines outside of public administration.[9] This
would suggest that while there is an interest in cross-disciplinary work
in the field of public administration, areas traditionally served by the
field of social work is not considered one of them. Nevertheless, Social
work scholars rue the 'take over' of public social services agencies by
professional managers (see Schorr 2000, for example).

Public administrationists and organization change theorists have
thoroughly examined the bureaucratic phenomenon in western culture
and its resistance towards innovation and change. This resistance is
due, in large part, to the pervasive domination of command and control
rule structures that affect every aspect of the modern human condition.
So inculcated are hierarchical forms into daily existence that we find
our organizational imaginations inhibited, stultified and, perhaps,
beyond reclaiming. At the bottom of the organizational food chain are
public agencies that have as their mission service to the weakest, most
disorganized and vulnerable members of our society.

Polsky (1991) claims that the bureaucratization of social services
was first conceived as a means for elevating and legitimizing local
charitable works. And, despite the warnings of a few skeptics about the
incompatibility of bureaucracy and casework, the desire to legitimize
prevailed. Today, the claims of these skeptics would be justified by the
realization that over half a century of hierarchical control and
formalized standards have culminated in a "rules-and-more-rules fetish
that has infected all aspects of program administration (179)." Such
organizations are in the most need of imaginative reconceptualizing.
The child welfare bureaucracy is a case in point. Casework with
children and their families requires a level of flexibility that rule-bound
structures simply cannot accommodate.

Particularly relevant to a discussion of child welfare discourses is
the work of organization theorists who contribute a psychoanalytic
perspective to our understanding of organizational life and the
behaviors of those people who are participants in it. Their emphasis is
on understanding organizational culture and the effects of the interactions of supraordinate and subordinate members. "Organizational
cultures are shaped by the leadership's personality and unconscious
expectations and demands. Frequently, leaders espouse one philosophy
and practice another (Diamond 1997, 65)." Diamond gives an example
of the leader and her assistants who publicly support a democratic,

participatory management style but are authoritarian in their approach to subordinates, a practice that they may not be consciously aware of.

Administrators may rationalize the need for an authoritarian (patriarchal) approach to protect the organization from the vicissitudes of its external environment; however, their greater fear may be loss of control. Unfortunately, in public child welfare agencies, leaders tend to come and go with some regularity, particularly when, as is often the case, they are political appointees. The instability created by frequent changes in leadership undermines employee initiative and productivity producing a fortress mentality that serves as protection against powerful, sometimes hostile forces at the top and outside of the organization. New initiatives like family preservation that require elements of risk-taking on the part of workers, supervisors, and administrators, as well as changes in those operating procedures that prohibit the flexible use of agency resources, are viewed by the organization's permanent staff with skepticism, fear of possible reprisals for missteps, and ultimately, hostility. These reactions are wholly predictable since, if the agency is to do its work, it must successfully accommodate frequent changes in leadership and staff, and the inevitable political intrusions.

## *Boxism and Seriality*

Social relations, characteristic of all forms of organization, are hierarchical but not necessarily static. As with families, the social relations of its members acknowledge authority and deference to authority, which are pragmatically functional behaviors. However, rigid social relations suspend possibilities for creative interpretations of the inevitable issues of daily life and depress the initiatives of subordinate members for devising and contributing creative solutions. A predictable result of rigidity in the social relations of organizations is 'boxism'. Farmer (1995) suggests that one of the characteristics of a postmodern view of alterity, the moral relationship with the other person, is a preference for diversity and that this preference is in contrast to the administrative boxism found in bureaucratic organizations. He explains that administrative boxism is illustrated in our propensity to label, or stereotype employees by their job title and their position on the organizational chart (228).

Public agency administrators and their counterparts in business and similar enterprises are both conscious and unconscious practitioners of boxism. An employee's first introduction to an organization is an explicit knowledge of her place on the organizational chart—the box she occupies, if she is privileged to occupy a box. Putting someone in her place and finding a place to put others is a central feature of organizing and reorganizing that can, in the latter case, be instrumental in positioning, repositioning, and eliminating workers for reasons that are often political, and self-serving. How we view ourselves in relation to the organization's structure figures prominently in our personhood and in our aspirations for our future and our expectations for others. Even those claiming a lack of ambition are acutely aware of their positions within the organization in relation to their peers, subordinates and superiors. Words such as peers, subordinates and superiors, conjure up vivid associations in the mind's eye and are symbolic representations of our personal worth and the worth of others. Even seemingly contented employees wrestle with the limitations imposed by these symbolical representations.

In the public child welfare system, the position that the caseworker occupies in the organization is twofold. She is a professional and an expert in the eyes of her clients. Yet, her role as professional is ambiguous intra- and inter-organizationally. Within the organization, her work is circumscribed by rules and procedures that may make little sense in relation to client needs, rendering her ability to act in the best interests of her clients difficult or impossible. Her relationship to other organizations in the helping community, including mental health professionals, physicians, attorneys and family court judges, to name a few, is often that of a subordinate, with a typically subordinated ability to influence client-affecting decisions. For example, her role in court proceedings involving her client is likely to be that of witness, not expert.

In response to boxism, the notion of seriality may be applied to the construct that we call public organizations, and more particularly to the child welfare agency, and the claims and prescriptions we make for the way they function. Iris Marion Young (1994) borrows Jean Paul Sartre's (1960) existential notion of seriality as a means for overcoming essentialist criticisms of the feminist project. Conceptually, according to Young, seriality acknowledges the multiplicity and diversity of associations that configure our relations with one another: personal, political, sexual, collegial, temporal, and spatial among others, along with the expectations we have of these relations. Its application to organizations has a liberating potential, the potential to free us from the patterns of behavior that are defined by the boxes we construct around ourselves and around others. We are all aware at some level of our positioning in our personal and professional relationships: we may live in the shadow of a spouse vicariously assuming their aspirations and accomplishments; children learn to describe themselves in relation to the social positioning of their parents; as we move through the stages from childhood to old age we trade on our assets and fear our inadequacies either as not-adult, not beautiful or handsome, not talented, not smart enough, or no longer young. Politically, we align with winners, or if with losers as the victims of winners. In the public organization, the relationship to power is as acutely felt as in private enterprise.

The public-private dichotomy in the matter of boxism is of consequence only in relation to the methods by which employees are eliminated. Once vested, the public employee is accustomed to tenure and a sense of security that is less reliable in the private sector. Conceptually, seriality offers a two-fold antidote to boxism: 1) by stripping away, if only temporarily, the categories that inhibit individuality and imagination, authenticating that which is submerged by false constraints; and 2) by acknowledging the multiplicity of categories that we use to define ourselves. Because nothing yet replaces bureaucracy in our collective consciousness our inhibitions to thinking beyond boxes stifles creative solutions to bureaucratically defined problems. In this, the public child welfare agency is a metaphor for public organizations, generally. And, in thinking serially, an artful response to bureaucratic problems need not be a contradiction in terms.

## Responding to Boxism

Boxism is a useful metaphor for discussing not only our propensity to stereotype people, but our inclination to categorize as extremist ideas that challenge mainstream practices. Most of us are aware of the problems associated with public child welfare organizations through news accounts or, perhaps, personal experience. The reasons given for their poor performance usually center on high caseloads, and a lack of services to meet the demands of their principal client base— disadvantaged, poor women and children. As noted in Chapter 1, public programs for dependent children are bureaucracies organized along traditional hierarchical lines with client services organized by function, for example, intake, general counseling services to families, foster care and institutional placements, and adoption services.

As we have suggested, a principal feature of the bureaucratic organization is its rigid adherence to rule structures. In the case of the child welfare agency, this structure is particularly ill-suited to the demands of troubled families and children. For example, the traditional child welfare worker customarily works an eight hour day, 5-day week (uncompensated over-time for emergencies is common). However, the times when client families are most likely to need the services of a caseworker are before and after school and work and in the evenings when caseworkers have gone home and the agency is closed. Bound by their bureaucratic discourse, child welfare agencies require clients to be present at meetings during traditional working hours creating hardship and added pressures, particularly for hourly wage workers who are least able to afford the loss of pay and are the most vulnerable to termination for missing work. For the organization that bases decisions about child placement on evidence of parental commitment, such inflexibility and lack of regard for its clients' precarious economic circumstances exemplifies boxism.

An artful response to the traditional work week, suggested by a University of Iowa union consultant (whose name we can no longer recall), is the 'extraordinary work week' in which social workers are personally accountable for their hours, using them as required over a seven day period. A more flexible use of time might enable caseworkers to meet with clients when the casework need is greatest. The hours that are not required for client services belong to the social worker, under this plan, to use, as with any personal time, as she chooses. Theoretically, client needs would be more readily met when the need is the greatest, and social workers would have greater flexibility in the use of their time—both on and off the job. Organizing for family centered practice demands a flexibility that frees workers from the boxes they inhabit in bureaucratically structured agencies; the extraordinary work week is only one example of how such flexibility might be accomplished.

The dominance of habit over the possibility of better practice often prevents administrators from seeking alternatives like the one we describe. Minuchin, Colapinto and Minuchin (1998) find it puzzling that ". . . the idea of the family as an interactive system doesn't resonate for [public agency] staff members, although many features of their own working environment apply to this other, smaller system as well. In particular, it should be obvious that the individual doesn't function independently, and that the effects of individual effort are unlikely to be sustained if the relevant system doesn't change (30)."

In 1911, Frederick Taylor (1947) described the functional foreman in *Scientific Management,* the work for which he is best known, as a replacement for the prevailing military-type structure in manufacturing plants. Taylor maintained that because the generalist boss could not command all of the knowledge necessary to contribute the required expertise to the specialized activities of each of his workers, the workers were not able to rise to their optimal potential and efficiencies were lost. By limiting the duties of the shop foreman to a single function for which he had special expertise, Taylor's workers would belong to different groups ". . . according to the particular functional boss whom he happens to be working under at the moment (99-100)."

The alternative management style that Taylor proposed was repeatedly rebuffed by the factory owners who hired him as a management consultant. The strength of the hold on organizations of a style of management, in this case, the military style, was so compelling that the owners were willing to forego potentially effective outcomes rather than alter shop floor practices. Taylor was practicing a form of 'seriality' when he suggested that employee relationships could be recast, reformed, and re-established even though they contradicted management practices of the time. He complained of the difficulties he had in convincing owners that his plan was in their best interests (and the best interests of the workers) citing a similar example of resistance in the work of Charles D. Rogers (Taylor 1947, 73). Rogers experienced equally stubborn opposition in his attempts to convince the owners of a Rhode Island screw works that child laborers could be made to complete their tasks more readily if they were freed to go home to play when their assigned work was finished (Taylor, 99). Although Taylor's plan is commonplace today, Rogers' idea (applied to adults in today's workplace) is still radical.

In recent years, public organizations have begun adopting some of the practices common to smaller entrepreneurial organizations and adapting them to much larger ones. More common now are organizing techniques like matrix management, project teams, and informal work groups that are designed to draw the best talents of individuals together to accomplish specific projects. Work groups and project teams, where one person may lead a project team while sitting as a member on another team, are commonplace in public agencies, although only infrequently observed in the child welfare community. Women, who make up the largest proportion of the child welfare workforce, remain subjugated in patriarchal bureaucracies that are ill-suited for their work, either unaware of, or powerless to adopt potentially liberating options for organizing their work.

Another theorist rarely invoked in public administration discourses is Antonio Gramsci (1971), an early twentieth century Italian intellectual, who referred in his Prison Notebooks (1929-1935) to the 'Taylorizing' of intellectual work. The context for Gramsci's proposal was a burgeoning industrial economy, a shortage of skilled labor, and an urgent need to train new workers—not dissimilar to the character-ization of many public child welfare agencies. His example was the work of newspaper editorial committees that functioned also as political cultural groups. In their collective discussion and criticism, each member brings to the table his particular expertise—raising the level of expertise of each to the most skilled of its members—"from which emerges an ever more select and organic collaboration." Gramsci writes that "...in this kind of collaborative activity, each task produces new capacities and possibilities of work, since it creates ever more organic conditions of work . . . (28-29)." His organic (thinking and organizing) intellectuals nurtured from among the worker class has an aspect of 'seriality'—which might be envisioned as a tapestry of affiliations.

A variant of organic collaboration is well suited to the public child welfare agency. Faced with unending complaints of abuse and neglect, and the concomitant problems of inadequate staffing, high turnover rates and new workers who are poorly prepared to treat complex family issues, something akin to organic collaboration might offer some relief. Clients assigned to collaborative teams of workers who share case plans and treatment strategies could have a mitigating effect on the problems associated with worker resignations and the ubiquitous transfer of cases. The group practice teaming concept has the potential to respond to the desperate need to train new and less well-trained workers. The child welfare community owes it to children and families, as well as to its own workers to find expedient methods for sharing the expertise that is both a valuable and often scarce commodity.

Experienced caseworkers, like most professionals, perfect their skills through years of continued work with their clients. Unfortunately for clients, rewards acknowledging one's professional acumen, mainly in the form of promotions and salary increases, generally require that social workers move up to supervisory and administrative positions with a consequent disengagement from direct client contact. It should be possible to reward professionals in the public social services agency for their skills as counselors and therapists by creating a parallel promotion system designed to give skilled caseworkers the option to continue working with clients. As it is, the principal avenue to advancement is through promotion to management.

Caseworkers, trained and experienced in family therapy, are a valuable asset in family centered practice; however, the public child welfare system is not designed to reward expertise in 'advanced' casework. It is neither difficult nor inappropriate to envision a parallel promotion track that would nurture and reward the development of this highly specialized area of casework practice—it is commonplace in organizations employing technical and scientific professionals. Leveraging such a notion in the state and local government personnel system would require administrative tenacity and a commitment beyond the will of most public child welfare executives. A remedy of this magnitude suggests the need to think radically beyond the limitations and confines of common administration discourse. And, it would help to have the community's support.

## Conclusion

The extraordinary workweek, team practice, and parallel professional reward systems suggest a rethinking of the relationship of workers to clients in bureaucratic child welfare organizations. Thinking serially demands that the inhibitions of boxism be overcome, and that the characteristic barriers that confine our thinking to habitual patterns, whether about the structure of organizations, or about our expectations for the people who inhabit them, be surmounted. It seems possible through this means to further explore and exercise the art of administration. Public social service agencies need both will and imagination to see the possibilities that innovations that challenge their bureaucratic constraints and risk-averse cultures can offer them.

The art of administration eludes the administrator whose role is circumscribed by boundaries that are seemingly impermeable to imagining beyond old habits and practices. Taylor envisioned the functional foreman as a method for increasing productivity by helping workers achieve their potential on the shop floor; however, scientific management's more appalling aspects have clearly overshadowed Taylor's objective. A reading of Taylor's original works reveals a clear interest in motivating workers and limiting the authority of managers to control workers by whim.

Schachter (1989) pursues a revisionist view of Taylor, suggesting that the textbooks that portray him as an unyielding, unfeeling autocrat are misinterpreting him and his work. Gramsci's fascination with 'Taylorism' was not to increase the wealth of factory owners, although he too, was interested in productivity. He was attracted to the potential for increasing the skills and sense of responsibility of workers to produce and organize work, and perhaps more importantly, to create from within the working class organic intellectuals capable of taking a leadership role in politics. Both Taylor and Gramsci illustrate an expanded view of seriality that challenges traditional boxism, and, at the very least, suggests the need to deconstruct closely held notions upon which much of our current organizational and administrative theories are based.

The threads of multiple discourses weave in and out of the public child welfare system, but there the analogy ends. The notion that the discourses we have discussed overlay and somehow make whole cloth of the system would imply that there is some master design or pattern, but this is clearly not the case nor can it be. It would be incorrect to suggest that a grand design is either possible or desirable. In fact, we suggest that the quest for such a plan has led us up a succession of blind allies with the result that much time, energy, and incalculable human and financial resources have been used up on schemes that yield little in the way of lasting change. What has developed out of the limited discourses of social work, family therapy and public administration, is a narrow child welfare discourse, focused on child saving without benefit of mentoring from the broader discipline of social work, or the therapeutic knowledge and skills of the family therapy movement. The child welfare discourse that has emerged from the vacuum left behind by social work has been strongly influenced by the executives and boards of directors of quasi-governmental, not-for-profit agencies and philanthropic foundations. There is little evidence to suggest that these organizations are better stewards of the welfare of children and families than the public agency.

---

## Notes

[1] Foucault, Michel ed. (1975) *I, Pierre Riviere, having slaughtered my mother, my sister, and my brother....* New York: Pantheon Books, p. 188. Paraphrased. Foucault refers to the peasant's loss of identity at the demise of feudalism and the subsequent rash of parricides in early 18th century France.

[2] Minuchin & Elizur draw from the work of J. Donzelot (1979) for their rendition of the story of la turret.

---

[3] La turret (the baby slot) has been resurrected in Germany according to an Associated Press story that appeared in the Houston Chronicle (Burt Herman, March 9, 2000, 18A). "The baby slot is located near a train station in the poor section of Hamburg. When a buzzer is rung, a door opens and a platform is lowered into a warm bed; a sensor alerts health care workers about 2 minutes later." According to the same article, a similar program has been in effect for 4 years in Budapest, and another in Johannesburg, South Africa.
[4] Ibid, pp.76-78
[5] Browning quoting Mary Parker Follett, p.16.
[6] Giovannoni, J.M. Telephone interview, July 9, 2000.
[7] Personal Interview with Salvador Minuchin, October 7, 1999, Boston, MA.
[8] The National Association of Social Workers (NASW) states that only about one-third of all professional social workers are employed by federal, state, or local governments, and that only about 28% of child welfare workers have a Bachelor's or Master's of Social Work. NASW Internet web site (www.naswdc.org/).
[9] (N=313)

# Chapter 4

## Responding to the Family Question: The Federal Children's Bureau

*Introduction*

Children were officially recognized as a responsibility of the federal government with the creation of the Children's Bureau in 1912. However, their families were the focus of policy only in so far as their capacity to parent was at issue. This was the case in 1912 and remains the case today. The federal government, through its agency designees, was, and continues to be a resource to the primary service providers which are the states and localities. Regulatory responsibilities of these federal government agencies are manifested in determining the rules for the distribution and use of designated funds and for the amount and distribution of certain discretionary money authorized by Congress for state services. Responsibility for the welfare of the child is scattered piecemeal throughout the social services system at all levels, national, state and local. This scattering became more pronounced in the mid-1960s with the proliferation of new programs and the dispersion of categorical programs, that is, programs designated to serve a particular type of client or client problem, for example, troubled youth and developmental disabilities.

In Chapter 3, we discussed conflicting discourses, suggesting that this could explain, at least in part, the difficulties experienced by advocates in garnering widespread support for viewing the family as the focal point for services, and family practice as a therapeutic alternative to traditional child welfare services. The federal discourse is, of course, multiple, and fragmentation of policy objectives is its inevitable product. The first half of this chapter briefly discusses the work of the Children's Bureau from its inception, with emphasis on the major changes that the Bureau experienced following several institutional reorganizations beginning in the mid-1960s. It was during this period that the most serious fragmentation occurred and the obvious opportunities to find a family focus were lost. In the second half of this chapter, we concentrate on the Bureau's response to family practice policies.

## The Children's Bureau

The original charge of the Children's Bureau was to study and report on the status of children. Specifically, the act establishing the Children's Bureau (37 Stat. 79) stated that the ". . . Bureau shall investigate and report. . . upon all matters pertaining to the welfare of children and child life among all classes of our people, and shall especially investigate the questions of infant mortality, the birth rate, orphanages, juvenile courts, desertion, dangerous occupations, accidents and diseases of children, [child] employment, legislation affecting children in the several States and Territories. . . (Bradbury 1956)." The bureau has never entirely surrendered this task, but over time, the burden of such study and reports has been shared with various national child advocacy organizations, sometimes cooperatively and sometimes separately, depending on the issue and political circumstances. A reading of the early history of the bureau suggests that it functioned much like the non-profit policy groups of today function i.e., problems were identified and studied, and study findings were shared with Congressional committees, which, it was expected, would address the problem through legislation and appropriation.

For the first fifty years of its history, the bureau was staffed mostly by professional women making it unusual among federal agencies.[1] That they were professional women whose principal concern was children may have been a contributing factor in the limited responsibilities and funding given by Congress to the bureau over the years. From its inception, the women of the bureau, recognizing this limitation and the precariousness of the bureau's Congressional support and funding, were cautious in choosing their battles, and in avoiding unnecessary political conflicts. Nevertheless, their careful research and tenacity in pursuing well chosen objectives led to important legislative initiatives, not least among them mother's pensions, and child labor laws. It was not until later in the bureau's history that conflict avoidance became more pronounced, and this because of systematic political intimidation within the agency, rather than from Congress.

The bureau was assigned administratively to the Department of Labor in 1913, where it remained until 1946. Between its establishment in 1912 and 1935, the bureau advocated for sufficient income to meet the basic needs of mothers (mother's pensions), maternal and infant medical care, childcare for working mothers, and child labor laws. Following the passage of Aid to Dependent Children (ADC) in the 1935 Social Security Act, and assignment of the program by Congress to the newly formed Social Security Administration, the staff of the Children's Bureau turned their attention to child welfare services in the states. Among these services was foster care (both family and institutional) for children whose parents were unable or unwilling to provide what was considered appropriate care, and services to assist poor and troubled mothers.

Between the years following the economic depression in the 1930's and World War II, the approach taken by Children's Bureau staff became more therapeutically oriented placing a greater emphasis on individual counseling and on the credentialing of professional staff, mirroring changes in the social work field with which the Children's Bureau staff were closely allied. In 1946, the bureau was assigned to the Federal Security Agency that was a part of the Social Security Administration. The Federal Security Agency became the Department of Health, Education and Welfare in 1953. Remarkable among federal agencies for their longevity, bureau personnel were considered serious professionals. Its chief, protected by the civil service system, was not subject to replacement by political appointees as was common in other agencies when presidential administrations changed. Whether or not this happy circumstance occurred by virtue of the bureau's particular standing with Congress and its largely female staff, the result was a continuity in leadership that was enviable among federal programs not similarly endowed.

The bureau worked actively with professional organizations, particularly medical and pediatric associations, and relied upon women's organizations (e.g., the Federation of Women's Clubs and local Child Study groups) to build state programs and support for them in state legislatures and Congress. There was active collaboration with private child welfare agencies, and especially with the Child Welfare League of America (CWLA) that represented private children's agencies. Bureau publications, usually written by staff hired to conduct research in house, were considered to be authoritative and were widely distributed to both professionals and parents. A particular strength of the bureau was its employment of child welfare specialists who were recruited for their expertise in particular areas of child welfare, such as adoption, foster care, protective services, and licensing. They were responsible for developing information and policy in their areas of expertise, convening meetings, conducting studies, making present-ations, responding to Congressional inquiries, and building constitu-encies that could be called on when action on a policy was needed.

Much of this work was conducted in collaboration with the CWLA, which employed similar specialists who served the private sector.[2] The bureau developed regulations for state agencies and the CWLA set certain standards for professional behavior; together they created the framework for action in the child welfare field. Although policy was specialist-driven, it was neither independently conceived nor arbitrary. Each issue was carefully studied in consultation with other bureau staff, and with members of professional organizations, university experts, and representatives of service agencies, both public and private, before a recommendation was announced. This arrangement had a salutary effect on the child welfare field with bureau professionals enjoying the considerable respect of their colleagues in state child welfare agencies, schools of social work and in the field, generally. All of this began to change during the 1960s with several major reorganizations and with the occurrence of the triple revolution: the civil rights and anti-Vietnam war movements and President Lyndon Johnson's war on poverty initiatives.

In 1963, the bureau was moved out of the Social Security Administration where it had been housed since 1946, and into the Welfare Administration of the Department of Health, Education and Welfare (DHEW). Four years later in 1967, another reorganization occurred that included the abolition of the Welfare Administration and the creation of the Social and Rehabilitation Services (SRS) of which the Children's Bureau was made a part. By 1968, the bureau included divisions on Maternal and Child Health, Child Welfare Services, Family Services, Delinquency and Youth Services, a research division, and a division for publications and reports. The office of the bureau chief included staff to manage national conferences as well as the regular meetings of the Interagency Committee on Children and Youth, and to serve as the principal organizers of periodic White House Conferences on Children. However, each of the administrative reorganizations that occurred during this period affected the bureau's work and its status as bureau programs were reassigned, staff moved, and responsibilities distributed elsewhere.

The sea changes that occurred in the United States as a result of the civil rights movement, the war on poverty and the anti-Vietnam war demonstrations also affected the work of the bureau. Although the specialists employed there generally approved of the policy changes that resulted from these public demonstrations many disapproved of the methods of activism used, considering them unprofessional. The administration of the war on poverty programs was assigned to a new agency, the Office of Economic Opportunity. When Richard Nixon became president in 1969, human services and education programs, including Community Services and HeadStart, which were war on poverty programs, were transferred to DHEW, which by then had experienced its own form of radicalization with periodic sit-ins in the Secretary's office.[3]

Between 1967 and 1969, the Children's Bureau was involved in a bitter internal struggle that involved the assignment of most of its programs to other agencies. For many participants and observers, these moves resulted in a profound loss of vitality and influence of the bureau's work, marking, for all intents and purposes, its programmatic death. All of the Maternal and Child Health programs were transferred to the Public Health Service located in Rockville, Maryland. Juvenile Delinquency and Youth Services were separated from Child Welfare Services and were eventually assigned to the Department of Justice. Child Welfare Services to the states remained in SRS. The Office of Child Development (OCD) was established in 1969, making a home for the HeadStart program, and the OCD director was given administrative responsibility for the Children's Bureau whose own chief was demoted to associate chief. The research division and the few child welfare specialists that remained from the original bureau were assigned to OCD along with HeadStart which dwarfed the bureau in funding and staff.

The only advantage that could be named from this reorganization was that the associate chief of the Children's Bureau, although now a political appointment, was considered so insignificant by the administration and those that followed it, that the position was either given to a professionally trained appointee or was left vacant. This allowed the deputy, a civil service employee, to manage the organization. Research funds were split three ways among the Bureau, SRS, and Maternal and Child Health. Child welfare training funds, a grants program earmarked for schools of social work, remained with SRS, as did the Child Welfare State Grants program. Both had been associated with Aid to Families with Dependent Children, which was now recast as a rehabilitation program, dispensing financial aid without benefit of the social services that were formerly a part of the program.

This separation received a mixed reaction in the social work field, some applauding the differentiation between social counseling and giving financial aid. Others lamented the split, noting that many AFDC families also required social services and would now have two workers rather than one. Following these reorganizations, the bureau was left with specialists in adoption, foster care, day care, licensing, and the odd new program that had no obvious home. Between 1967 and 1969, the Children's Bureau staff was reduced from 400 to twenty.

The professional social work culture of the old bureau was greatly altered with this latest reorganization. Prior to these changes, the Children's Bureau was noted for its formality. Only titles and last names were used, and there was a strict adherence to chain of command. Social events were conducted as formal teas. In the debate over reorganization, the bureau staff were characterized as inflexible, and the professional staff whose average age at the time was fifty-eight, was derided for their social work counseling approach. For example, when criticizing a grantee the program specialists followed a counseling-type format: there must be two or more positive statements followed by a 'suggestion' that some change should be made, followed by another positive statement. In criticizing this approach, one project officer was said to have questioned whether or not the object of the criticism actually realized that he or she had a problem. The therapeutic administrative style was probably less offensive to the new culture resulting from the triple revolution of the 1960s, than was the formal behavior of the older professional women of the Children's Bureau. To the urban social revolutionaries of this new period, these older women who seemed so resistant to change, represented the very culture they wished to reform.

The confrontational style of community activists that was so offensive to their elders in the bureau was quickly replaced by more tempered management styles; but by this time, most of these elders had retired, been transferred elsewhere, or had left the agency. In the meantime, the administrators of HeadStart, one of the premier war-on-poverty programs, sought to avoid the perception of being a program for problem children by resisting pressures to take a stand on social problems. The OCD leadership did not want HeadStart to become a social welfare treatment program despite the growing body of research that suggested that child neglect and abuse might be present among this population.

The battle over the placement of the HeadStart program is described in detail by Gilbert Steiner (1976) in the *Children's Cause*. The association of these programs and child abuse and neglect with the old Children's Bureau and the antipathy with which the bureau's staff accepted the reorganization no doubt had some influence on the OCD decision. This attitude changed over time with the result that HeadStart doors were opened to handicapped and developmentally disabled children, homeless, and foster children, although there was never a coordinated approach to dealing with their problems.

In the meantime, the crucial role of the child welfare specialist had been seriously undermined. Although some of the same people remained in the newly reorganized agency, the infrastructure that supported their work no longer existed. Instead, specialists became coordinators. Access to the resources of the agency and support from the agency administration was insufficient to maintain their status as national experts and attempts by specialists to exert their expertise was viewed by some administrators as a challenge to administrative authority.

Beginning in 1968, with the appointment of a new research director, studies that were once done by specialists inside the agency were contracted out using cooperative agreements (vaguely specified contractual arrangements) principally with the Child Welfare League of America. The league, in turn, subcontracted to a small, rather select group of university researchers. While these individuals and their universities were well respected, there was a clubbiness about the process that engendered rancor among those not in the group. After 1970, announcements on funding priorities were issued by the agency, and research and demonstration projects were awarded to a broader representation of outside groups, among which were local and state government agencies, private organizations, and universities. The federal project officers that were assigned to monitor these grants were of varied educational backgrounds and only a few were social workers. Because these new project officers had access to outside information and experts, they became *de facto* competitors with the older specialists who had remained with the agency following its reorganization.

In 1970, Frederick Green, a pediatrician, became associate chief of the Children's Bureau with Frank Ferro as his deputy. Although Green left in 1973, Ferro, with a masters in social work and experience in community organization and juvenile delinquency, continued alternately as deputy or acting chief until 1982. During this time, he began rebuilding the bureau. Considered by his staff a creative and demanding administrator, Ferro pursued four general objectives during his tenure: 1) recovering the child welfare services program from the Social and Rehabilitation Services; 2) renewing support for state child welfare agencies; 3) using research and development projects as a vehicles for identifying new program models and disseminating information about them to the field; and, 4) establishing the National Center on Child Abuse and Neglect pursuant to the Child Abuse Prevention and Treatment Act passed in 1974.

The assignment of responsibility for state child welfare services to SRS was considered an unfortunate compromise in the bitter disagreement among the administrators who established OCD, and DHEW had the authority to undo the decision. Nevertheless, state child welfare services were not returned to the Children's Bureau administration until 1978, ten years and two administrations after the unit was assigned to SRS. Although SRS had responsibility for child welfare services in the states, its principal programmatic focus was the Aid to Families with Dependent Children program. This left many of the child welfare services in the states without the technical assistance they'd become accustomed to from the old Children's Bureau. The ten regional DHEW offices employed specialists in child welfare mirroring those in the bureau (foster care, adoption, protective services, and licensing) and the Children's Bureau staff in Washington were determined to work with them to provide more direct help to the state agencies in their regions.

Without state child welfare programs, the Children's Bureau really had no clients. Although the staff still considered themselves spokespersons for all children, they had little more than their publications to prove it. One option for reclaiming its prior role was through the strategic use of the discretionary funds that were annually assigned to the Office of Child Development (OCD) for distribution to contractors and grantees in furtherance of OCD (and Congressional) goals. Another option was seeking out new programs that served new populations, a function of the discretionary grant program. The Children's Bureau was an agency seeking a mission.

Prior to its first reorganization, the bureau had worked with agencies providing services for unmarried mothers. These services focused on medical care and residential services during a young mother's pregnancy, since adoption was assumed to be the service goal. Before the civil rights movement, these programs served primarily low-income white women. Women who wanted to keep their babies generally dropped out of school but remained in their communities, and services for African-American women were few to nonexistent (Billingsley and Giovanonni 1972). Recognizing that the majority of young mothers were not receiving an education, a demonstration program was funded, which, when it proved successful, became a model for dissemination. The successful model provided child care services, making it possible for young mothers to remain in school. Conferences were organized to acquaint educators and professional groups with the program, a successful strategy that became the norm for promoting other new programs.

Another initiative, begun in 1972, encouraged the adoption of African-American children. Social service agencies serving African-American and minority children were funded to promote adoption through training conferences for African-American social workers and community leaders. Edward Ziegler, the first Director of OCD in 1970, initiated another important program. Although his principal interest was in HeadStart, he was also concerned that young people should receive parenting education while still in school. He arranged funding to develop and test a curriculum for youth that contained information about babies and young children including hands-on involvement with children in child care centers. The resulting curriculum, "Education for Parenthood" was promoted nationally.

In 1971, the Children's Bureau was once again reorganized as the National Center for Child Advocacy. During this brief period, the bureau also began promoting a public administration approach among child welfare agencies by directing funds to administrative studies in schools of social work. While the advocacy emphasis, at least in name, was short lived, this pattern of program development continued. New program models were developed and disseminated using research and demonstration grants with the professional conference as the principal vehicle for disseminating information to the field. Over the next ten years until 1981, the bureau managed to rebuild itself.

## *Initiatives Directed at Child Abuse and Neglect*

In 1972, Senator Walter Mondale conceded failure in his attempts to pass legislation for child care programs for all children, and instead turned his attention to the claims of Dr. Henry Kempe, Dr. Ray Helfer and others who were advocating for legislation to address 'battered baby syndrome'.[4] The bureau's research division funded several grants to study the child abuse problem. The American Humane Association was awarded a contract to design a national reporting system in order to understand the extent of the problem and a demonstration grant established 'Parents Anonymous', a parent support and treatment program.

When Secretary Caspar A. Weinberger took office in 1973, DHEW was ordered to develop an agency-wide plan on how to address the national problem of child abuse. Top agency officials met several times without noticeable result until the head of the budget office identified $4 million and ordered each sub-agency to plan the use of its share. Eleven demonstration programs were jointly funded by the bureau and SRS and an evaluation of these programs was funded and managed by the Public Health Service.

The Office of Education (still a part of DHEW) and the National Institutes of Mental Health also funded demonstration projects that addressed child abuse from their perspectives. Agency wide involvement and coordination occurred with annual meetings involving all projects and their project monitors. Before the second year funding was due, the National Center on Child Abuse and Neglect (NCCAN) was established by Congress as a part of the Children's Bureau, and SRS and the Public Health Service (PHS) both requested that the new center pick up the funding for subsequent years of the demonstration program. The bureau was successful in fending off this request; however, the resulting resentments created poorer relations for the bureau, especially with SRS, and caused considerable anxiety and uncertainty among grantees about the security of continued funding.

Secretary Weinberger attempted to head off the Child Abuse Prevention and Treatment Act (CAPTA. Public Law 93-247) legislation, enacted in 1974, arguing that current DHEW programs were adequate. However, the separation of children's programs between SRS, OCD and PHS, and a lack of specific focus on children's issues hampered his ability to make an effective case before Congress. CAPTA established the National Center on Child Abuse and Neglect

(NCCAN), which became another division of the bureau with staff drawn from other offices and the civil service list, few of whom had training or experience in child protective services. While the head of Family Services in SRS had insisted that child neglect be included along with child abuse as a responsibility of the program, neither protective services nor in-home specialists were transferred from SRS to the new program. The new director was Douglas Besharov, an attorney who had been council to the New York State Senate Committee on Child Abuse, an acceptable choice to the Republican Administration.

There was at this time no agreed upon theory as to either the causes or treatment of child abuse and neglect. Medical professionals focused on the identification of battered baby syndrome, a diagnostic term coined by Kempe in 1961, but did not attempt to identify the social and psychological causes that led to its manifestation. Abuse of older children was attributed to parental discipline that got out of hand, alcohol abuse, mental illness, and overstressed single parents, among others. Children with mental and physical disabilities were identified as potential victims. Neglect was associated with low parental intelligence, lack of education, inadequate income, social isolation, depression, abuse of alcohol and other drugs, among others. With so many potential causes and no theoretical framework for situating the problem, programs were funded with little regard for studying the larger issues of family violence. Research on the family at this time was safely lodged in universities and could be described as the sociology of the families of college sophomores.

The American Humane Association's new national registry project had one measurable outcome, an exponential increase in the number of child abuse reports, investigations and foster care placements. There was a 123 percent increase in reporting between 1976 and 1982, when over 900,000 reports were received, or about twenty for every 1,000 children. A 1977 national survey estimated that 502,000 children were in out of home care, up from 177,000 in 1961 (Shyne and Schroeder 1980). It was thought at the time that since national reporting and investigation requirements were mandated that states would respond to the increased workload by authorizing additional workers and programs. However, they did not anticipate the lag between the recognition of need and the time it would take to lobby their legislatures for appropriations to meet the need. State and local agencies were caught off guard by the number of children and families reported, could not keep up with the volume, and found that out of home placements were preferable to the potential danger presented by an unserviced child abuse case. Furthermore, the federal matching funds to the states for foster care placements was not capped making it less expensive to place a child out of home than to provide services to families in their homes.

## Prevention Initiatives

During this period, the bureau funded two programs that received national attention: one was the Nashville, Tennessee Comprehensive Emergency Services (CES) program. CES became a model for managing resources and coordinating the activities of the police and social services to expedite services to families experiencing crises and to prevent the placement of children in foster care after business hours (Burt, 1976). The other was the Oregon Permanency Planning project that coordinated social services and judicial intervention for the purposes of expediting termination of parental rights for children in foster care who could not be reunited with their families. In 1974, the Oregon Children's Service Department submitted a request to the Children's Bureau for demonstration funding to free children for permanent homes. Oregon had been removing children from abusing or neglecting parents at a high rate and wished to place those children considered adoptable—under twelve years old, not seriously handicapped, and unlikely to return home. This required adequate case documentation to convince the court that parental rights should be terminated. The bureau funded the project with Portland State University as the evaluator. Procedures were established, handbooks developed, and children were successfully freed. However, 26 percent of the children who had been designated as unable to return home, were actually returned to their parents (Emlen 1978). This outcome prompted the agency to consider alternatives to placement strategies, one of which was in-home, family-based services.

Following a search for strategies to disseminate information about these and other program models, the bureau awarded a five year contract to Mott-McDonald Associates, a local Washington, D.C. consulting firm, to identify, describe and promote a range of 'exemplary' programs. This million dollar contract resulted in the Child Welfare Resource Information Exchange (CWRIE). The CWRIE, with a staff of about fifteen, identified model child welfare programs, publicized them through a quarterly newsletter. CWRIE paid the program developers to give technical assistance to local and state agencies interested in adopting their models. It also conducted colloquia of experts on emerging areas of interest, for example, adolescent pregnancy prevention and adolescent suicide, from which papers were produced and disseminated. Although considered successful, the exchange contract was not renewed or re-competed. The reason for this is unclear. There apparently was some dissension between the contractor and the Children's Bureau; and, it is possible that the project threatened to become more visible than the Children's Bureau itself. After all, it could be argued that the project was doing exactly what the bureau itself should have been doing. In any case, the desirability of information dissemination approach was clearly positively demonstrated.

At this point, the bureau had three ongoing program activities: adoption, foster care, and child abuse and neglect. After CWRIE was discontinued, three sets of national resource or training centers were funded in the ten DHEW regions along with one devoted to Indian Child Welfare. A combination of child welfare research and development funds and NCCAN funds were used to support these thirty-one centers, most of which were located in university schools of social work. Although these centers were not formally evaluated, it appears that they worked well. About $17 million was shared between the centers and other research and demonstration projects, a large investment by bureau standards. During 1982 and 1983, Dorcas Hardy, the new Assistant Secretary for Human Services in President Ronald Reagan's first administration, zeroed in on these programs, claiming that they represented an unwarranted intrusion into state government, and despite protests written by state directors, the assault on the national centers continued. The centers did not charge fees for their services and publications, which might have reduced their operating costs. Also, the centers were thought to be building a political base and this was considered an inappropriate use of federal funds, although there is no apparent basis for this concern in the center materials reviewed for this work.[5]

By 1980, the activities of the child welfare specialists in the bureau depended on their ability to work with the project directors of these specialized centers, outside researchers, and the project officers of the internal research division. The bureau had become a more conventional government agency, taking direction from the DHEW administration and its own directors rather than from professionals in the field. Its scope was broad but its direct responsibilities remained limited. Also in

1980, landmark child welfare legislation, the Adoption Assistance and Child Welfare Act of 1980 (Public Law 96-272), was passed.

Implementation in the states of the permanency planning initiative begun by the Oregon project was slow going and child welfare advocates were convinced that true permanency planning would not occur without legal incentives and the involvement of the courts to insure that explicit safeguards were in place to protect the rights of children and parents. The new law required six month case reviews for children in foster care, explicit safeguards to insure that children were placed in the least restrictive environment (meaning that foster family homes were to be used before institutional placements were consider-ed), and court supervised eighteen month dispositional hearings.

The act reflected a profound distrust of the public agency and the professionals who worked in them to effectively do their jobs in behalf of children in foster care. It could be said that this distrust was warranted given the lackluster record of many, perhaps most, public child welfare agencies in the U.S. However, the failure of child welfare agencies to deal expeditiously with the vastly increasing number of child abuse complaints and with due process issues, could have been anticipated by observers who witnessed the exponential increase in abuse and neglect reports in the states after the 1974 Act was passed. Reactive public policy is common in the social services; policy makers do not respond with money until a crisis has occurred, and often, not even then.

The child welfare advocates that helped draft Public Law 96-272 also included a clause requiring 'reasonable efforts' to help families avoid child placement, or if placement was unavoidable, to make reasonable efforts at reunifying children in foster care with their families. At the time that it was drafted, advocates did not specify what services could constitute reasonable efforts and listed examples that had been used in the earlier Social Services Title XX of the Social Security Act. None of these were family focused services. The bureau acted quickly to develop detailed regulations for Public Law 96-272, addressing some of the omissions in the legislation. However, the incoming Reagan administration withdrew the draft regulations, issuing in their place a very limited interpretation of the act.

The principle of joint planning, that is the development of a state child welfare plan by the state and the regional representatives of the bureau, was retained but was attenuated by limitations on regional office travel funds. In addition, most efforts at technical assistance were interdicted, travel authorizations were curtailed and publications produced by the bureau were eliminated. Efficiency-making under the Reagan administration by the Office of Human Development Services (OHDS) was reinforced by the report of The President's Private Sector Survey on Cost Control (known as the Grace Report after the project's head, J. Peter Grace) which was distributed to OHDS senior staff in April 1983. The section on Management recommended that the Office of Families in ACYF be eliminated, and that "Training and technical assistance activities throughout HDS be limited to those defined as the 'continuing Federal assistance role' . . . [and that] All technical assistance activities currently being performed. . . which are not accordance with the Assistant Secretary's policy should be discontinued."[6]

## *Family Policies and Programs in the Children's Bureau*

Families exist only on the margins of United States child welfare policies—never achieving much prominence and with only a shadow presence in the minds of those whose focus is on services to children. From the beginning, the Children's Bureau's recognition of the family unit was limited to supporting mothers in rearing their children by offering advice on parenting, support for maternal and child health care, and by documenting the need for mother's pensions. The issues, roles, and responsibilities of fathers in the parenting relationship were generally absent. The bureau employed protective services and in-home service specialists to support in-home casework for mothers or homemaker services for father and children in the mother's absence (discussed below). The term 'in home' was used to differentiate these services from foster care and did not refer to family counseling.

Family and marriage counseling was the purview of the private Family Services agencies which, by tacit agreement between the Family Service Association of America (FSAA) and the CWLA, divided their responsibilities accordingly. The authors of an unpublished manuscript prepared by the Child Welfare Resource Information Exchange (Mott and Lunsford 1979), argue against separate designations of child welfare and family services since, "in defining child welfare services, the Child Welfare League includes *reinforcing* [italics ours], supplementing, or substituting for 'functions which parents cannot perform fully', while the FSAA describes its member agencies' purpose as '. . . to contribute to harmonious family inter-relationships, to strengthen the positive values of family life, and to promote healthy personality development and satisfactory social functioning of various family members.' (5)"

The authors of the paper reason that, "The main goal of child welfare services is the promotion of child welfare, and this may well mean the promotion of the family as a unit. Any attempt to separate the needs of each must be viewed as artificial, at best (6)." By the late 1980s, the Child Welfare League had adopted 'family preservation services' as part of its member objectives; however, FSAA has remained silent on the subject, perhaps because they view their members' work as having been family based from their inception.

The homemakers of homemaker services tended to be women who were trained to help families when the mother was incapacitated for some reason, or when the child needed special attention because of some handicapping condition. They were not considered professionals and usually worked under the supervision of a social worker. Homemakers were known to have assisted working mothers during the great depression and World War II. The National Committee on Homemaker Service proclaimed at their 1960 conference that the service was 'a community resource for families' and published a directory with the names of 303 agency programs in forty-four states. Participants saw a bright future for the homemaker.

Unfortunately, this was not to be the case. After the DHEW reorganization of 1968, the program received only limited support from Social and Rehabilitation Services (SRS), and none from the Children's Bureau. Although the homemaker programs were inexpensive in comparison with alternatives like foster care and professional counseling, they did not enjoy the status of the professional social worker and had few advocates in the professional community.

In the early 1970s SRS, which oversaw state child welfare grants, funded several 'family centers'. One such program was the Bowen Center in Chicago, a child abuse treatment project. The Children's Bureau, which was then part of the Office of Child Development, funded another program called the Extended Family Center that was located in California. Both were long-term (the families they served remained for several years) and expensive, and were not considered 'model' programs for dissemination purposes for these reasons. In retrospect, it appears that the successes that these programs achieved were not adequately reported.

An Office for Families was established under the Administration for Children, Youth, and Families (ACYF) in 1979, in preparation for the first White House Conference on Families in 1980. This new interest in families was motivated by politically conservative elements of the Carter administration (1976-1980) and reinforced under the Reagan administration (1980-1988). However, the same problem that hampered the distillation of family policy in the past plagued the people in these administrations: What exactly is a family? The more conservative groups sought a traditional definition of family as a heterosexual married couple with children by birth or adoption.

Unfortunately, the children who require the services of child welfare agencies are frequently members of single parent households and, with or without the need for welfare and social services, were a growing segment of the U.S. population in the 1970s and 1980s. These families, as well as the (at the time) wholly unacceptable homosexual and lesbian couples who also referred to themselves as families, were too controversial to figure, even on the margins, of the 1980 White House Conference. Another conference on Youth and Families, which did not evade these controversial definitions, was finally held in Colorado in an effort to distance itself from the spotlight in Washington. The level of conflict around these meetings was sufficient to deter further discussion of family legislation.

Back in Washington in February 1979, the Office of Families issued a "Report of the ACYF Family Task Force" which was distributed within the Office of Child Development. The background statement in the report indicated that no specific national policies addressed the well being of families; however, not surprisingly, many other policies directly or indirectly exert unpredictable, sometimes unintended and often profound influences on basic family functioning. Most obvious are programs directed at specific circumstances, e.g., developmentally disabled children, teen parents, runaways, abused and neglected children.

Although the language of the sixteen member task force report was milder than our own, it implied that in focusing on these specific circumstances, parents have been villainized, their weaknesses exploited, and opportunities for rehabilitating families, whenever possible, have been lost in the passion of child saving. Child welfare policies aimed at preventing foster care placement or at reuniting foster children with their biological parents were viewed as family policy in the report. Policies that focused on youth development mentioned families as part of problem resolution, and those that focused on early childhood development had an expectation of parental involvement and parental support. Child abuse and neglect programs mentioned family treatment as at least one objective.

Those policies cited in the report that indirectly affect family well-being and quality of life included on the job training, job finding, income stabilization, health services, housing, and education among others. There was no attempt to analyze these policies for their unintended effects on families. Recognizing the variability of American families, the report of the Family Task Force ended with a list of five goals for ameliorating this oversight, one of which was to dispense information to strengthen and support families, and another to expand the agency role as family advocate. However, the Office for Families was not established in law, had only limited funding, and, given the pending presidential election, was in precarious circumstances. What funding was available for distribution to grantees was proposed as a research and development priority entitled, "How to Get Services to Families" which amounted to several small one-year demonstration grants. The so-called 'Grace report', referred to above, cited the Office of Families for elimination, "because the unit has no program responsibility (80)."

The Family Impact Seminar, also a product of this time and thinking, was initiated following discussions by the U.S. Senate Select Committee on Children, Youth and Families, which was chaired by Senator Walter Mondale. The seminar was charged with the task of identifying the ways in which laws and programs negatively affect U.S. families in order that such effects might be moderated.

The seminar, which was funded by several philanthropic foundations, was begun with considerable optimism. Headed by a former Select Committee on Children, Youth and Families staff member, A. Sidney Johnson III, the seminar prepared several impact statements but, as time passed, it became obvious that there were serious methodological problems with operationalizing 'family impact'. Almost every law has some impact on families, and even a selective analysis would require a larger staff than the seminar's funding allowed. The organization drifted over time into a child and family advocacy group, doing useful work although not distinctive from other child advocacy organizations.

Definitional problems paled in comparison to the debate over the extent to which government should be involved with families, with issues of privacy and self-determination leading the argument in opposition. Child welfare surfaced in the national consciousness only rarely during the history of the Children's Bureau. The child labor issue caused debate in the early years of the bureau. The naming of juvenile delinquency as a national problem, followed by the official recognition of child abuse—associated in the minds of the public with battered child syndrome—all attracted national attention. However, nationally, child welfare issues have been background noise debated in earnest only by those with direct involvement in the field. The political conservatism that made an issue of defining family values began during the Carter administration and greatly intensified under the Reagan administration. Although consensus could not be achieved on the exact nature of 'family values', conservatives' emphasis on them made it possible for family practice advocates to obtain federal funding for family-based child welfare programs.

Separate and apart from the short-lived Office of Families, the Children's Bureau issued an announcement for a competitive grant to establish a national resource center on family based services in January 1981. The grant was $250,000 a year for three years and was awarded to the University of Iowa School of Social Work. Although not made clear in the stated objectives, the background discussion notes in the grant announcement indicated that the new center would assist states in implementing the pre-placement and prevention of foster care services required in the 1980 Adoption Opportunities and Child Welfare Act (Public Law 96-272). The Iowa School of Social Work had been funded in 1978 as a Clearinghouse on In Home Services, and Clearinghouse staff were actively engaged in promoting family practice with an ecological therapeutic orientation. The new Reagan administration appointees made clear their strong opposition to government intervention in families, which they considered social engineering. Despite this, it was possible to argue that family centered social work was a politically conservative goal.

The Heritage Foundation had reviewed federal programs for the new administration and issued an analysis related to each government department. 'Soft', or social science, research was in the crosshairs of the ideologically motivated minions of the new administration, with proposals to drastically reduce the budgets for most federal agencies. Social research was taboo; evaluations of social programs were sharply curtailed, and the Department of Health and Human Services[7] declared that it was not in business to support "studies of large scale social conditions or problems (Holden 1984)." Dorcas Hardy, the new Assistant Secretary for the Office of Human Development Services, the division that housed the Children's Bureau at this time, set to work on what many civil servants perceived as a search and destroy initiative.

For example, the rather extensive publication program of the agency was viewed as unnecessary since most of the agency-produced books and reports for and about children and families were said to be in competition with commercially produced publications. Therefore, the bureau's publication program was discontinued. Reports developed by grantees were considered the property of the grantee and therefore, should be published and distributed by the grantee, not the government. Since most grantees had not included publication and dissemination items in their budgets, many grantee reports were lost to public view.

The grant process was streamlined to reduce the paper work required of applicants, and the applicant review process was altered to eliminate the appearance of a politically liberal reviewer bias. So-called liberal reviewers were replaced by conservative reviewers who were personally approved by Hardy. The cooperative agreements with the Child Welfare League of America were terminated, and the League was eliminated from future competitions—at least for the duration of the Reagan administration. For most grants, funding was limited to seventeen months without renewal.

A flurry of small, one time only grants were made during this period—with no effort to strategically disseminate information about them. Neither were there any attempts to evaluate them. Longitudinal studies begun prior to Hardy's tenure were terminated quickly followed by a firestorm of criticism from the professional community. Coalitions of hitherto unaligned groups of scientists were organized to mount a campaign to stop the administration's wholesale gutting of research programs, and the threatened damage to long-term databases without which the government's information infrastructure would be seriously undermined. Fortunately, they were successful, having over the years developed strong bipartisan support in Congress (Holden 1984, 1052-53).

Hardy and her colleagues in the administration reacted by redesigning the grant-giving process, with the result that Hardy's strategic talents, once redirected, were used to create a well-organized and controlled coordinated discretionary grants program. A single announcement was issued by the agency that included requests for proposals across programs, and the application process became more detailed. Training grants directed solely to schools of social work were now open to other disciplines, for example, law, public administration, psychology.

Training in grant writing was offered by the regional offices in order to open the process to new potential grantees. Specific instructions were issued to federal employees to include the term 'and family', or its equivalent when referencing children. The Office of Families was reinstated; several staff were assigned to it and Jerry Regier was appointed as its new director. Regier was a former campus minister with strong views in opposition to divorce, abortion, and cohabitation, and like many of the Administration's appointees, had no experience in a government agency. Under his direction, a number of grants were awarded to community agencies with the recommendation of conservative reviewers and the personal approval of Assistant Secretary Hardy. Although the grants function itself was improved, the grant-selection process suffered from politically motivated favoritism.

Dorcas Hardy insisted on personally approving each grant reviewer, and each grant awarded by the agencies under her direction. She was also known to have had grants re-reviewed to obtain a higher ranking to ensure their funding. After a time, complaints by staff about this 'personalized' grant system caused an investigation to be conducted into the applicant review process in 1983 by the U.S. House of Representatives Intergovernmental Relations and Human Resources Subcommittee.[8] After reviewing the evidence, a report critical of Hardy's activities was issued, noting that she had used the agency's grant process as a personal fund for awarding grants to friends and to ideologically 'correct' organizations. Despite these claims that brought into question her suitability for the post, Hardy was appointed Director of the Social Security Administration. Subsequent administrators, heeding the unfavorable notoriety of Hardy's apparent improprieties, took pains to insure that the grant review process was a fair one.

During Hardy's administration, no particular interest was shown by the assistant secretary in the substance of services for families aside from the term's inclusion in ACYF publications. Agency staff were intimidated by the administration and were loath to make comments or suggestions about programs unless they were specifically requested to do so. In her second year as assistant secretary, Hardy announced that no multiyear programs would be continued without sufficient justification. A successful justification was written for the National Resource Center on Family Based Services by Susan Weber, the Children's Bureau Division Director, and the center was allowed to continue.

In subsequent years, the bureau's discretionary grant announcements included requests for demonstrations related to family-focused services including family-based Native American projects. The concept of family focused services was always of interest to tribal social services that did not find the concept at all radical. These projects were jointly funded by the Administration on Native Americans and the Bureau of Indian Affairs and a National Indian Child Welfare Center based in

Portland, Oregon. The center later became affiliated with the family based center in Iowa.

Also during Hardy's administration, a meeting of the National Resource Center Directors, numbering nine at this time, was called by the Children's Bureau urging them to become self-sufficient by charging for their services. Prior to this time, centers had offered information and technical assistance to state and local agencies without charge, since center staff salaries and travel were funded by DHHS grants. The goal, according to Hardy, was that the centers become self-supporting and the implication was clear: at expiration of the current grants, the centers' funding would be drastically reduced. This news was particularly distressing to the National Resource Center on Family Based Services staff, since it was still in the early stages of introducing state agencies to family based services. Furthermore, few of the center directors considered themselves marketers, most having come to their current positions through direct service agencies or universities.

Given this new entrepreneurial emphasis, center staff chose foster care prevention as its principal argument for convincing state and local agencies (which were also feeling the financial pinch of an economic recession and program funding cut-backs) that family based services were the best response to the Adoption Opportunities and Child Welfare Act of 1980 preplacement prevention requirement. Although foster care prevention had always been a center piece in persuading agencies to adopt family based services, the claim became a principal marketing tool in the self-sufficiency race, and its political inflation as a cost-saving device was, in the end, more damaging than helpful to the cause of family preservation.

The staff at the National Resource Center on Family Based Services was not without an ideological position. The original applicants for the Clearing House on In-Home Services, the forerunner of the resource center, had strong ties to Families, Inc., a program situated in West Branch, Iowa that used an eclectic, family systems model of therapy. It was one of the early family therapy programs serving public child welfare clients. Clearing House staff published two edited books that described the different family practice programs known to them at the time[9]. In neither of the books did the authors attempt to analyze the programs presented, and in almost every case, contributors were extremely enthusiastic about family based services. The terms most frequently used were community based, home based, intensive, and family empowerment. The authors' unabashed enthusiasm was not shared by staff at the Children's Bureau.

A New York program, evaluated with a grant from the bureau, and reported by Jones, Neuman and Shyne (1976) in *A Second Chance for Families* found that intensive services (defined as limited caseloads) were not very effective. It seems that workers spent excessive amounts of time on case management activities—trying to access the system, to get Aid to Families with Dependent Children (AFDC) grants or other services for their clients—and that the actual in-person time spent with families was relatively limited.

Based on that evaluation, the bureau funded seven demonstration grants to test whether the intensity of services might be a critical factor in the prevention of foster care placement. Although the intention was to fund similar programs for comparison purposes, the review panel was not made aware of this objective and recommended programs with the greatest variation among them. Furthermore, an evaluation design was not a part of the grant requirement, nor were the grants monitored in sufficient detail to make a summative evaluation practical. The seven grants cost over $3 million, and no empirical evidence as to the utility of intensive services was collected.

## The Bureau's Other Placement Prevention Programs

The bureau funded a number of 'prevention of placement' programs with decidedly mixed results. For example, the New Mexico Department of Economic Security applied for and received a grant to train all of their state workers in family based services and, although most of their workers were trained, no family based services were actually implemented in the state. Training workers was not helpful, it was discovered, if the system itself was not altered to accommodate new skills and practices. Such alterations were considered unfeasible by most agency administrators.

Homes for Black Children in Detroit was funded to develop appropriate services for African-American families, and to train public agency workers to work with African-American families. The agency was not able to obtain the cooperation of the public agency, which limited the success of this effort. The Phoenix Indian Center demonstrated that urban Indian families responded to the 'talking circle', an adaptation of a traditional form of family support. The Illinois Department of Children and Family Services conducted a very promising demonstration on preventive services for African-American families in public housing using an African-American agency.

However, the state's program managers showed no interest in the program and it was discontinued.

The Virgin Islands Department of Social Services won a small grant to train their workers; however, bureaucratic restrictions prevented the newly trained workers from practicing what they had learned. The Family Based Resource Center trainers lamented that they had never before worked with staff so eager to learn. The Puerto Rico public agency also received a 3-year grant to train workers. This project continued for five years on a 3-year grant and continued to send progress reports to the bureau as the program was expanded statewide. Minnesota, one of the earliest states to initiate family based services in their public agencies, was also funded to expand their family services program state-wide and were considered successful in meeting this goal.

The Department of Health and Human Services initiated a joint funding relationship with the Edna McConnell Clark Foundation of New York to support a placement prevention project in Delaware, and a training program for judges at the National Council of Juvenile and Family Court Judges. Both were considered successful. Following an interagency agreement between the Bureau and the National Institutes of Mental Health, the Missouri Department of Mental Health, the Office of Developmental Disabilities and Mental Health of South Dakota, the Cambridge/Somerville Mental Health Association in Massachusetts, and the Denver Indian Health Board were given grants to develop intensive family services.

These projects were more expensive than the average grant to state social services departments because staffing costs were higher. The projects had difficulty working out interagency agreements with mental health and social service agencies. In Massachusetts, establishing interagency agreements consumed the first year of grant funding. In South Dakota, the attempt to provide Homebuilder-type services on a Native American Indian reservation was viewed as competitive with other state efforts and furthermore, the approach was not well received by Indian families. However, the Denver program, also a Home-builder's model, achieved good results by using principally Native American staff. Unfortunately, most of these programs ended when the funding did. The Missouri program was the exception. It was quite successful and, with considerable assistance from an energetic and tenacious advocacy organization, became the foundation for a state-wide family centered program. The Minnesota program, with a historically strong family-based tradition, is still in place at this writing.

In addition to these projects directly funded by the Bureau, the National Resource Center on Family Based Services worked principally with public agencies in most of the United States. Between 1981 and 1985, the center staff worked with agencies in twenty-two states. After 1985, the number was considerably reduced along with the center's federal funding for technical assistance. The promises to keep foster care in check using family-based and family preservation services were difficult to demonstrate during this period.

An economic recession in the 1980s was accompanied by a reduction in real income, job losses, drastic decreases in low-cost housing, an escalating use of crack-cocaine, the spread of the AIDS epidemic among poor women and their children, and increases in juvenile violence. Furthermore, state legislatures were not funding public child welfare services at a pace necessary to keep up with burgeoning caseloads. All of these events conspired to greatly increase foster care caseloads.

There was another complicating factor during this period: the American Civil Liberties Union (ACLU) Children's Rights Project. Since 1979, state child welfare agencies and those serving large urban areas had been the target of the ACLU's Children's Rights Project which brought class action suits against them in behalf of children languishing in foster care. Although the project, under the direction of Marcia Robinson Lowry, had good intentions—to force public child welfare agencies to comply with the 'reasonable efforts' provisions of Public Law 96-272—the consent decrees resulting from these law suits tended to immobilize agencies, diverting workers from case work to paper work. Compliance with consent decrees so encumbered these agencies that adopting new programs was, for most, out of the question. Of course, it could be argued that the agencies that were the focus of these lawsuits were probably the least likely to try something as radically new as family preservation services.

## Conclusion

The bureau's early history was marked by successes that have had significant long-term impacts on the health and welfare of children and families in the United States. Until the 1960s, when its highly regarded work began to suffer from internal fragmentation, too frequent reorganizations, and the loss of many of its resident experts, it was an authoritative voice of professional child welfare. From that period until today, the bureau has struggled to provide minimal assistance to its state child welfare agency constituents—the significance of this loss is becoming only a dim memory since most of those involved before the bureau's downhill slide, are gone.

Even in its heyday, the bureau's work centered on the child with very little interest in the family unit. Although family preservation was recognized by the bureau in the late 1970s, serious efforts to re-think child welfare practice to accommodate family could not have taken place in the atmosphere of paranoia that enveloped the bureau during the Reagan administration. The fact that the Children's Bureau has continued to win internal agency support for the re-named National Resource Center on Family Based Practice through four presidential administrations and more than fifteen years indicates to us that the concept remains an important one.

The constraints under which the advocates inside the Children's Bureau labored have been significant. Hostile Administration appointees, the failure to fund sound research and evaluation studies that would provide empirical guidance to policy makers in Congress and the states, and the constant reorganizations and consequent undermining of child welfare expertise among the agency's few remaining specialists, has rendered the bureau largely ineffective. The vacuum that is left has been filled by private, not-for-profit, national organizations—it is presumed, by political design—further fragmenting child welfare services and severely limiting opportunities for public discourse, a topic we discuss in the next chapter.

Adoption and foster care (including kinship care—in which children are placed with relatives rather than strangers) remain the principal programs promoted by the federal government, to wit, the Clinton administration's pressure on Congress to facilitate the speedier adoption of children (Adoption and Safe Families Act of 1997). Nevertheless, the majority of families that are served by local agencies are not at risk of child placement, at least not at the time their case is initially opened. Services to these families are both minimal and predictable.

---

## Notes

[1] The Department of Labor Women's Bureau, created by Congress June 5, 1920, was the only other organization staffed principally by women.

[2] CWLA is a private, not for profit membership organization established in 1920, to set standards for and disseminate information to its member

organizations that were, until recently, principally multi-service private, nonprofit child welfare agencies. (http://www.cwla.org/)

[3] John W. Gardner was DHEW Secretary from 1965 to 1968. Wilbur J. Cohen, DHEW cabinet secretary from 1968 to 1969, was replaced, following Richard Nixon's election to the presidency in 1969, with Robert H. Finch. Secretary Finch held the office until 1970, when he was replaced by Elliot L. Richardson. Richardson remained in office until 1973, when he was replaced by Caspar W. Weinberger. Secretary Weinberger remained until President Nixon's resignation in 1974.

[4] See Kempe, C. Henry & Ray E. Helfer. 1972. *Helping the Battered Child and his Family.* Philadelphia: Lippincott.

[5] Hardy, Dorcas. Memo in relation to "report of the President's Private Sector Survey on Cost Control," p.80, June 5, 1983.

[6] Hardy, Dorcas. "Task Force Report on The Department of Health and Human Services Department of Management, Office of Human Development Services and Action," p.80. The President's Private Sector Survey on Cost Control, April 15, 1983.

[7] DHEW became DHHS in 1980.

[8] News Release, 99th Congress, Committee on Government Operations, May 7, 1986. See also: Kellam, Susan, "Senate Postpones Hearings on Hardy Nomination", *Federal Times*, May 12, 1986, p.3.

[9] Maybanks, Sheila & Marvin Bryce, eds. (1979). *Home-Based Services for Children and Families: Policy, Practice and Research.* Springfield, IL: Charles C. Thomas, and Bryce, Marvin & June C. Lloyd, eds. (1981). *Treating Families in the Home: An Alternative to Placement.* Springfield, IL: Charles C. Thomas.

# Chapter 5

## The Advocates: Multiple Discourses

### Introduction

We find that the common view of advocacy—the view that advocates practice apart from the public, private and quasi-public organizations that constitute the formal service bureaucracy—does not apply. We find instead that advocacy discourses are present in all of the elements that constitute the child welfare system. Therefore, our construction of child and family advocacy must necessarily be a broad one. It includes the actions of individuals and the *ad hoc*, grass roots organizations that work to alter the circumstances affecting the well-being, the quality of life, of children and families. It also includes national non-profit membership and non-membership service organizations that are part of the institutional structure of the child welfare system as well as institutional activists who are members of government organizations that set policy and provide direct services to child welfare clients. We also add to these groups, philanthropic organizations that identify with social movement activism and consulting organizations, both for profit, and not-for-profit, that act as external change agents.

There is a certain nobility to the advocate, something like Plato's gadfly, which, Socrates claims, . . . arouses, persuades, and reproaches, and in so doing is a gift to the state (25). At its best, advocacy works for positive changes in ailing and stagnant systems, altering old notions of what is right, correct, good, at least in the present. Advocates may also anthropomorphize organizations, imbuing them with the properties of a disdained competitor in a contest where winning becomes a personal mission. For some, the element of challenge, the game, excites their interest. Victories, even small ones, won at the expense of established interests, are as seductive as the failures that reinforce the advocate's convictions about the system's faults. For the individual advocate, there is no professional code of conduct that sets boundaries of behavior and, as Paul (1977) suggests, this ". . . absence of givens, rules, or boundaries is the Achilles Heel of the advocate and the potential lance of the system the advocate seeks to change (142)." Nonetheless, advocacy is a fundamental element in participatory democracy, and at its best, functions as conscience and heart in the body politic.

In our discussion of child welfare advocacy, we consider the roles of government and private institutions, consultants, philanthropic organizations, individuals and the grass roots organizations that they create to give voice to their collective interests. Child welfare discourse has been shaped by the advocates who have influenced many of the changes made in the area of child and family policy in the United States. In this chapter, we examine advocacy discourses and their relationship to the adoption of family centered programs and policies in the nation's child welfare system. Following a discussion of advocacy types, we examine examples of family based advocacy, highlighting the particular approach to social program marketing used by the Edna McConnell Clark Foundation of New York.

## Advocacy Discourses

Those that participate in our loosely defined conception of advocacy are members of a complex web of organizations with motivations that we consider to be facilitative, persuasive, entrepreneurial, and altruistic in nature. Facilitative advocacy involves linking clients with services (Lourie 1972), services with other complementary services, information with service providers and policy makers, and funding with program developers. We view facilitation as a largely non-partisan form of advocacy in which the client, the family in this case, is both the motivation for and recipient of the advocacy effort. Lourie suggests that this is an appropriate role for governments. Persuasive advocacy, on the other hand, is ideological in nature, akin to the single-issue interest group, is partisan, and often passionate. Facts may become exaggerated; hyperbolic discourse is not uncommon, and participants are inclined to polarize around a set of issues. "Ours is the best, or only course of action" is the motivating discourse and losing ground on an issue is seen as a defeat.

Although grass roots organizations are inclined to persuasive advocacy, they are by no means the only participants. National non-profit organizations that lay claim to a particular ideological stance and that are vocal advocates for a position are persuasive advocates. Entrepreneurial advocacy is linked more closely to one's personal livelihood with motivations that are less easily distinguishable between the welfare of the end-recipient (client) and one's professional status and future. Finally, altruistic advocacy is transcendent, and is inherently unselfish and non-self-involved. We believe that altruistic advocacy is a guiding principle for many individuals and groups. However, altruistic advocacy can be compromised when organizing becomes formalized, and tensions around funding and personnel issues, among others, interfere with mission and vision.

Facilitation, persuasion, entrepreneurialism, and altruism are discourses, not categories or boxes. In our view, the groups we discuss engage in all of these discourses, although the pattern of discourses for some appear to be more heavily weighted in one area than in the others. We hypothesize that these discourses are practiced in multiple arenas that may be characterized by their level of influence on public policy.

Advocacy is exercised both formally and informally in public and private organizations. Some government agencies, the Children's Bureau, the Administration for Native Americans, and the Administration on Developmental Disabilities are examples, have as their mandate advocating the welfare of their ultimate constituents—children, in the case of the Children's Bureau. Despite their detractors, particularly among political conservatives who regard this role as inappropriate in government, and despite periodic, politically motivated sieges that use reorganizations and diminished funding to dampen their influence, these, and similar organizations, continue to be a public voice for the marginalized.

Individual workers in public and private child welfare organizations advocate for the families and children on their caseloads, often bucking the system to obtain material goods and services for their clients. Sometimes, the efforts of individuals rise to the level of institutional advocates (Santoro and McGuire 1997). For example, we recall the story of a worker in a New York city public agency in the early 1970s whose resolve to locate appropriate housing for a single mother and her physically handicapped child contributed to the development of an interagency case planning group which became a model for multidisciplinary case management, nationally.[1] This group included, among others, the housing authority that was finally pressured into producing a subsidized apartment in a building with an elevator through the persistence of the family's caseworker. Although both the federal agency role, and that of the planning group in our example, engaged in facilitative advocacy discourse, the discourse of the worker whose tenacity so impressed her colleagues could be described as altruistic. Her efforts transcended the facilitative. She pressed the limits of the system and made it work in behalf of her client—and ultimately, many others.

National non-profit organizations, for example, the Child Welfare League of America, the American Public Human Services Association, and the Young Lawyers Division of the American Bar Association, assume an advocacy role when working for their members and, by extension, the children and families that their members serve. Other social mission-oriented organizations, the Children's Defense Fund and the American Humane Society's Children's Division come to mind, assume a more direct advocacy role, collecting data, issuing position papers, and presenting testimony before Congress in behalf of children.

In 1981, the Child Welfare League issued a "Statement on Child Advocacy" taking the position "that *any* contemporary social agency cannot be simply a service provider. It must also be concerned with the inseparability of general child welfare policies, issues, and principles, and the direction of its own policies, practices, and advocacy in each of these areas (1)." The statement also underscores the responsibility that public and private (or voluntary) child welfare agencies have to be persuasive advocates in behalf of children with different facets of the political system by virtue of their unique position in the community. Persuasion is powerful discourse when engaged in by organizations with respected member-constituents or led by charismatic individuals armed with empirical evidence in support of their cause.

Consultants with incomes derived by performing services to child welfare agencies, are another group that figure prominently in child welfare advocacy. As purveyors of information, new techniques, and knowledge, they seed the child welfare landscape, sometimes with flowers, and at times with weeds. Often viewed by agency employees with deserved skepticism, consultants as professional outsiders, nevertheless contribute to the debate with their prescriptions for change. Included among the many organizations that employ consultants, are small firms created around a single major federal contract, the large national accounting firms that diversified to include the design and installation of information management systems and management consultation, universities and private institutes that train child welfare agency employees, and the various policy, research and resource centers funded by the Children's Bureau and philanthropic foundations.

The Child Welfare Resource Information Exchange (CWRIE), a federal contract awarded to Mott-McDonald Associates, a private, for-profit consulting firm based in Washington, DC (mentioned in Chapter 4) supplied the funding that kept a small fleet of consultants busy identifying and disseminating information about 'exemplary' child welfare programs from the mid-1970s until the contract and the firm expired in 1980. CWRIE, staffed principally by social workers and sociologists who worked closely with Children's Bureau specialists, is an example of the facilitative function of advocacy that consulting can perform. It did what the Children's Bureau seemed unable to do. It located programs (before the advent of the Internet) that were described as innovative by sources in the government, among advocacy organizations like the Child Welfare League of America, and by word-of-mouth; some programs were the products of federal grants.

The center widely disseminated the information using a newsletter and mailing lists gathered from child welfare membership organizations. CWRIE was the forerunner of the various information dissemination grants, which were called resource centers, that were subsequently funded by the Children's Bureau and which adopted many of the same dissemination techniques that the first resource exchange had used to good effect.

Community Research Associates of New York, directed by Bradley Buell (discussed in Chapter 2) is another example of consultants as advocates. Buell and his colleagues worked with the St. Paul Family Centered Project during its formative period, pressing the project's participants to adopt Buell's particular theory of service monitoring and forecasting (called case finding) that was based on the prevalence of indicators of family maladjustment. Community Research Associates was engaging in entrepreneurial discourse. They advocated for families using theories they were actively marketing to other agencies that were also paying clients and that were contributing to the organization's income.

Another arena of influence not generally associated with advocacy is the philanthropic foundation that achieves its policy ambitions by encouraging grantees to conform to program objectives through strategic grant-making. Silver (1997) notes that the foundation studied for his research viewed its actions and identity as social movement activism rather than philanthropy. Whether a foundation's principal identification is social activism or philanthropy, it is clear that several large foundations have used their considerable wealth to influence child welfare policy at both national and local levels. An example of this persuasive approach to social activism is described in an article featuring an interview with Peter Forsythe, then Vice President of the Edna McConnell Clark Foundation of New York.

Money, according to the article, is used as a strategy as well as a gift to achieve bottom up reform by seeking out creative leaders, organizations and agencies that are willing to shape broader social policy. Specifically, Clark's Children's Program, led by Forsythe, supported the Homebuilder's behaviorist-learning model of family practice, called it family preservation, and described it "as a specific, definable, in-home, short term service which has been shown to prevent placement of children in out of home care (1)." This is a particularly powerful statement coming from the vice president of a foundation that spent an estimated \$40-45 million[2] over a decade in pursuing its family preservation policy objectives.

U.S. citizens in the twentieth century, unlike other industrialized nations, have witnessed the influence that individuals can have on public policy through the sheer might of fabulous wealth. Although philanthropic foundations have been criticized periodically as tax dodges and threats to the national tax base, the effect of their persuasive powers on public policy has received less attention in the scholarly literature or the popular press (Hall 1992; Lemann 1997). Certainly in the instance of child welfare policies, money grants have had a particular power to influence, given child welfare's chronically impoverished state.

Mannes (1993) and Adams (1994) credit the financial support and strategic planning of the Edna McConnell Clark Foundation, and Peter Forsythe, for the rapidity with which family preservation gained influence in child welfare policy. The success of the social marketing approach used by Clark, was, according to Adams, neither an indication that the model the foundation marketed, Homebuilders, was superior to others, nor that the foundation was particularly conspiratorial in promoting the model:

In the context of the Federal retreat from the field and cash-starved public agencies, the logic of marketing indicated the strategy Clark followed. Following this logic made success possible with a relatively modest, in relation to total child welfare spending, infusion of funds. No more sinister motivation need be sought than the desire to focus the foundation's resources on what its leaders concluded was the best available model, the one which offered the most relative advantage and the best promise for wide dissemination. (Adams 1994, 428)

Although those who were not among the privileged grantees may disagree with Adams's characterization of the Clark foundation as guileless in pursuit of market advantage, they would likely agree that without the concentrated infusion of funds and technical expertise, and with sole reliance on anemic federal initiatives, family preservation would not have achieved policy status as quickly as it did. We will return to this discussion later.

Among individuals, advocacy motivates people with similar interests to come together in groups, *ad hoc*, or formally organized with a constitution, by-laws and tax exempt status. Common at the state and local levels, these organizations are viewed with ambivalence by traditional child welfare agencies as both the means for conveying informally, information that the agency is unable for political reasons to share with the public, and as a thorn in the side when criticizing agency policies. Whether kitchen table advocates or sophisticated policy analysts, grass roots groups have been significant contributors to child welfare discourse. Local advocates, those closest to service providers and their clients, have been a force at times in directing the conversation, and at other times in spreading the ideas and convictions of pioneering professionals to a broader constituency.

## Advocacy for Children and Families

In the early 1980s when family preservation was becoming more widely known and the Children's Bureau was experiencing another retrenchment, several grass-roots organizations were persuading their respective state agencies to adopt family preservation services with compelling arguments about cost-savings in foster care as the hook. Kansas Action for Children, a coalition of civic and service organizations is an example. The coalition sponsored conferences and workshops, contracting with the state social services agency to purchase consultation in family preservation services in the state's behalf, when the state was unable to authorize the purchase directly.

A similar grass root group, Citizen's for Missouri's Children, used a different approach. Advocate, Phyllis Rozansky, who spearheaded the Missouri effort, used her expert analytical skills to create technical reports with the state's child welfare and budget data. These professionally crafted technical reports became very persuasive tools in seeking, and securing policy alternatives to foster care. As with other special interest groups, advocates for abused and neglected children have organized, the better to be heard and to influence the direction of child welfare policy. Such organizations create the infrastructure that transforms individual voices into collective action. However, the success of advocacy organizations depends on their members' ability to attract the attention of policy makers, to enlist their support, and to convince them that the cause is both politically feasible and politically advantageous.

Organizations that represent children and that are national in scope tend to be conservative advocates, that is, their brand of advocacy is institutionalized. It is our view that they recognize the need to secure, reinforce and maintain their positions without jeopardizing their standing in the community of professionals. They adopt a predictable conservatism when faced with experimental programs and innovations. Yet these same organizations may be influenced to adopt a paradigmatic shift if there are sufficient incentives, for example, federal or foundation grants. Such grants appeared to have motivated ideological changes toward the family preservation 'Homebuilder's' model in several prominent child welfare organizations, namely the Child Welfare League of America, the American Public Human Services Association, the Children's Defense Fund, and the National Association of State-Based Child Advocacy Organizations (Adams 1994, 422).

When prominent organizations that are trusted to provide leadership in their fields endorse one program over another, policy and practice are bound to follow. Since empirical evidence for the efficacy of the family preservation models are contested (see Chapter 6), their choice to support the Homebuilder's model was strongly influenced, we suspect, by funding opportunities.

Mannes (1993) describes family preservation as a professional reform movement, spurred by the realization on the part of professional social workers that the child welfare system was failing children and their families. He cites a series of studies[3] indicting the foster care system for its failures to return children to rehabilitated families or to the permanence of adoption, noting as compounding factors, legislation that created financial incentives (Title IV-A of the Social Security Act) to place children in foster care, and a growing foster care population. We dispute Mannes's notion of a professional movement and suggest, instead, that those who formed the movement represented multiple discourses, and that the traditional social work organizations, the university schools of social work, and the National Association of Social Workers, were among the last to join. Those who did were often working at the margins of the social work profession, many of whom were, in fact, disdainful of social work's inertia in dealing pro-actively (to use a social work term) with the problems of a dysfunctional child welfare system.

Professionals, inside their respective professional boxes, are constrained from overt advocacy in most cases by very valid fears: losing opportunities for advancement, losing opportunities for interesting assignments, and losing their jobs. As Hartman and Laird (1983, 18) note, many of the social workers engaged in the family therapy movement saw themselves as family therapists first. However, advocates outside the organization perform an important role for the institutional advocates on the inside, particularly those who are marginalized in their own professions. They can speak publicly to those in power, administering Plato's 'sting' to the state. Paul, Neufeld and Pelosi (1977) describe the child advocacy movement that they believed was occurring at about the same time that the family preservation movement, described by Mannes, was getting its start. According to Paul:

> Child advocacy is a growing social movement that speaks not only to the need to provide more effective integrated services, a message most all acknowledge and support, but it also speaks to the need to defend the child against services, no matter how well intended, that favor the interest of the system at the expense of the child. This is the message we are willing to listen to but find very difficult to hear. (Paul 1977, 5)

How are the child welfare and family preservation movements connected? Only tangentially, and that is where the tragedy lies. The multiple discourses that characterize these movements have kept them separate although it should be clear that the power and influence of one would increase the power and influence of the other. The philosophical basis for the family preservation movement and its emphasis on family rather than on the individual child, is in helping families to exercise control (empowerment, if you will) over their behavior towards one another and their environment. This is the basis for self-advocacy. With the ability to assert some control over one's life, one may also advocate for one's children—with the school, the physician, the mental health professional, social workers, and others who, as Paul suggests, wittingly or unwittingly favor the interest of the system at the expense of the child.

In earlier chapters, we described a child welfare system that is disconnected from other community helping systems, and in general disarray. We have suggested that by organizing services around the family rather than the individual, this disconnectedness would be minimized, and that systems that currently seem to be working at cross-purposes might be integrated to serve clients to better effect. However, child welfare advocates more often than not view family preservation as promoting the rights of parents over the rights of children, citing incidences of maltreated children who were returned to abusive parents (or the abusive live-in boyfriend of a single parent mother) and were subsequently re-abused, or killed (Berliner 1993, 556).

There is clearly substantial cause for concern when children are returned to abusive caretakers without benefit of intensive treatment and close monitoring. Certainly some children should *never* be returned to their abusers—indeed, it would be foolhardy to suggest otherwise. Yet, institutionalized neglect is a continuing problem in the child welfare system. Advocates in both 'movements' acknowledge that family preservation policy cannot be imposed on organizations that do not have the financial and human resources to do it right. However, family preservationists suggest that if these resources are available in adequate measure, many, perhaps most, families can rear their own children. Missing in this advocacy network are those whose discourse involves a macro view of organizing. There is no anti-bureaucracy (boxism) movement as such, although there are those in the field of public administration who question the efficacy of bureaucracy as the best principle for organizing ourselves (Farmer 2000), not the least of which is Max Weber, the so-called 'father' of bureaucracy. As Farmer notes, bureaucracy's cost is high, trading the spirit of our humanity for the iron cage of rationality (Farmer, 77). (See Chapter 3 for a more complete discussion of this view.)

## *Examples in Mental Health and Developmental Disabilities*

Child welfare advocacy is similar to mental health advocacy in that neither group's needs nor interests are easily definable. For both groups, the needs that are defined are contested and the contesting groups are unwilling or unable to mediate a unified course of action. Chandler (1990) suggests that competing advocacy interests, that is, the medical versus the legal interests of mentally ill persons, have created an imbalance in the mental health field This imbalance which has been created by disagreements and tensions in the mental health advocacy movement, is contrasted with advocacy in behalf of the developmentally disabled. Chandler notes that the deinstitutionalization of developmentally disabled persons was accompanied by policies that insured that community support was in place for individuals leaving the hospital. "The family members of the developmentally disabled person, in concert with professionals, attorneys, and politicians forged an effective coalition to provide for these handicapped persons and insure their safety with public money (114)."

The unifying element in the successful advocacy for developmentally disabled persons appears to have been the active involvement of parents. Parents advocating for their offspring are a powerful force in the community. Without parental involvement, or when parents are viewed as dysfunctional and their behavior as causal, advocacy is left to surrogates. Surrogates, whether social workers, attorneys, physicians, mental health professionals, or adult survivors of the system, represent a particular stance—each of which sees the child, or the mentally ill person, through their particular, socially (professionally) constructed lens. Professionals may share the public's tendency to view the protagonists in this drama with suspicion. Mentally ill persons or their parents are suspected of having caused the illness, the parents of the abused and neglected child are suspected of being bad or mentally ill, and the abused or neglected child is viewed as damaged.

## *Federally-sponsored Family Advocacy*

The Child Welfare Services Program of the Community Services Administration formally recognized family based services, albeit unwittingly, when a child welfare training grant was awarded in 1978 to the School of Social Work at the University of Iowa for an in-home services information clearing house. (The grant was moved to the Children's Bureau for supervision later that same year.) The stated purpose of the clearing house was to disseminate information about in-home family based programs, which were considered by Children's Bureau staff to be homemaker services. This type of service employs paraprofessionals whose original role was to help out when a family's homemaker was hospitalized or died and until other arrangements could be made. More recently, homemakers have been employed to help neglectful mothers learn parenting and housekeeping skills. However, the first director of the Clearing House, Marvin Bryce, had just completed his doctoral dissertation on the Families, Inc. program of West Branch, Iowa. This program with its combination of family therapy and the more homespun tasks of hands-on parenting education, or modeling parenting[4], became the template for the Clearing House's information dissemination, training and technical assistance activities.

Employees of the Clearing House established contacts with national child welfare organizations and state agencies, conducted workshops and presented papers at child welfare conferences, held their own conferences and workshops, collected and disseminated information about programs, wrote papers and books and produced materials that were convincing in their praise of the family based program model (the term family preservation was not used by the center). In so doing, they were able to persuade Children's Bureau staff that in-home, family-based services could usefully serve as an alternative to the over use of foster care for neglected children. At this point, less attention was paid to the problems of families implicated in child abuse, principally because less was known about the effectiveness of family therapy for family members who exhibited violent behaviors. Many of the programs that had achieved therapeutic successes with poor and dysfunctional families routinely rejected families with a history of family violence or overt substance abuse, circumstances frequently present among abusers.

Marvin Bryce and his associate, June Lloyd, with the aid of School of Social Work faculty, wrote the winning proposal for the first National Resource Center on Family Based Services, awarded to the University of Iowa in 1980. This grant expanded the work of the Clearing House to include technical assistance to six state child welfare agencies over a 3-year period. A review of the National Resource Center's quarterly report to the Children's Bureau for the period January 1 through March 31, 1984, indicated that within four years of the grant award the resource center's professional staff were working in some capacity with nineteen state agencies while participating in conferences, publishing training materials, a policy manual, a state training plan, a directory of programs, and a newsletter. Between 1981 and 1990 the Children's Bureau funded the National Resource Center on Family Based Services at about $250,000 a year, increasing this amount to accommodate several subcontractors and ancillary projects in the late 1980s.

There is no question that the work of the Resource Center generated interest in family-based services. It is also clear from reading the center's quarterly progress reports to the Children's Bureau, that substantive changes in these states moved slowly, or were stillborn, the victims of diminishing resources, administrative changes, more pressing priorities, and a lack of will to correct structural impediments to family practice. A principal impediment to the acceptance and implementation of family based practice was, and continues to be the notion that the family should be the locus of service delivery. As we noted earlier, the social definition of family is contested, but more to the point, the legal definition of family does not as yet make allowances for non-traditional families. Family, it appears, is too politically charged to be either the locus of service or the focus of advocacy.

## Family-Based Services Advocacy Organizations

Following the first national conference devoted to family based services in Minneapolis, Minnesota in the early fall of 1987, a national family based services association was formed. At the time this organization was begun, a schism among family centered practice advocates had developed. On the one side were those who supported or were practicing a family systems or ecological[5] approach—the approach promoted by the federally funded National Resource Center on Family Based Services at the University of Iowa. On the other side were advocates of the Homebuilders, Inc. program, a behaviorist model based on social learning theory that was begun in Tacoma, Washington in 1974. It was the preferred recipient of grants that were made by the Edna McConnell Clark Foundation to replicate the Homebuilders program in other localities.

The first members of the national association of family based service providers were involved principally with the University of Iowa resource center. The association's members tended to have had some experience with the center, either through technical assistance provided by its staff, or as participants in conferences and workshops sponsored by the center. Initially using a national conference as its core activity, providers, professionals and family based services advocates used the association as an opportunity to share their practice experiences with one another, learn from experienced, nationally recognized family therapists, and broaden the family practice discourse to include multiple visions of family practice.

Several years after the association was formed, members began to complain about the incursion of the Homebuilders organization into their states—lobbying state legislators, state human services managers, faculty in university schools of social work. They perceived an imbalance in access to funding resources between the non-Homebuilders, and the Homebuilders' programs but were helpless to do anything about it since the funding resource was private. It was becoming clear that the Edna McConnell Clark Foundation was using its considerable wealth through strategic grant making to influence public policy at the statehouse level toward the exclusive support of the Homebuilder's program over those programs that subscribed to other family treatment approaches.

Although Clark's approach to marketing the Homebuilder's program was remarkable in the experience of child welfare advocacy, Clark was simply part of a general activist trend among philanthropic foundations. Tax exempt foundations are statutorily prohibited from lobbying. They were, nonetheless, becoming more involved in influencing political and legislative outcomes for social and political change through a process of strategic grant making. Lemann (1997, 18) suggests that the 1969 Internal Revenue Service ruling that foundations must give out annually a fixed percentage of their assets, and the stock market-related growth in these assets, resulted in more ambitious giving beyond charitable good works. Although foundation activities may not be overtly noticeable, strategic grant making achieves the same ends as lobbying without public interference or oversight.

## The Clark Strategy

The Edna McConnell Clark Foundation's Vice President and Children's Services Director, Peter Forsythe, an attorney by education, was experienced in state-level social services administration and as a national advocate for the adoption of children with special needs. Through his position in the foundation, Forsythe provided the national-level leadership that was lacking in the federal government, a position that created envy among others in the child welfare field—and resentment, principally among those who were not included in the 'inner circle' of his associates. His exclusive focus on the Home-builders program created additional resentments, since no other organization, government or private, was funding family based practice at the level lavished on family preservation. Probably most resented was his apparent single-minded strategic approach to marketing family preservation as a national policy, in many cases, overlapping and ultimately overshadowing the earlier work with state agencies and legislatures of other family based service advocates.

The Clark Foundation initiated its Children's Program in 1972; Peter Forsythe was the program's first director. In 1983, the foundation gave a grant to the Child Welfare League of America to identify model programs for the prevention of foster care placement[6]. According to Children's Programs Director, Susan Notkin, ten programs were identified and in 1985, a network of foster care prevention programs was initiated. Criteria for inclusion in the network were that services be provided in the home, be short-term and intensive, serve families whose children were at imminent risk of foster care placement, and provide both 'hard' and 'soft' services. (So-called hard services include helping a family apply for food stamps, finding a working refrigerator, day care, or a job. Soft services are counseling and therapy.)

Although the network was not a cohesive one and failed to gel as a group, the effort was not considered a failure since, among the group, one program stood out over the others. That program, Homebuilders, Inc., of Takoma, Washington, seemed to have the "clearest set of program values regarding what they did with their families," according to Notkin. And from this revelation, the Clark staff and consultants determined to put the foundation's money behind the program in which they had the greatest confidence that their prevention of foster care goal would be achieved. Accordingly, they began to strengthen the capacities of other programs to develop and replicate the Homebuilders model.

The term family preservation was coined as the defining program characteristic, and the marketing effort to make it a national child welfare priority was launched. The foundation sought 'Homebuilders states', and gave small, strategic planning grants to state agencies in Iowa, Missouri, Kentucky, Tennessee, New York, New Jersey, Connecticut and Minnesota. Leadership development programs were funded with the Child Welfare League of America, the National Conference of State Legislators, and the National Council of Juvenile Court Judges.

Data was required to make the case for family preservation. In addition, it was needed for the National Conference of State Legislators who annually produced information on the number of children in foster care for their members. The Center for the Study of Social Policy in Washington, D.C. was funded and staffed by child welfare policy experts who had prior professional experience in state and federal child welfare organizations, for the purpose of conducting studies and preparing briefing papers that supported Clark's family preservation initiative.

Small, strategic grants were made to existing professional and advocacy organizations with experience in information dissemination, professional development, training and technical assistance to state and local child welfare agencies. Several joint programs were initiated with administration officials in the Department of Health and Human Services, although limited and tentative, since trust between the two organizations was not at a high point. The general ineptitude of administration officials who were not a source of expert knowledge, was generally understood. A network of academics was initiated, which produced scholarly papers, presented at professional conferences, and promoted family preservation among their colleagues. During this period, Forsythe was meeting with strategic-ally important executives and policy makers in the child welfare community, in professional organizations, the Congress, and state legislatures. In other words, the Clark foundation had the area covered, and was much more committed and persuasive in pursuing their objectives than the Children's Bureau was capable of being.

It could be argued that true strategic planning was not, and is not possible in the organizational atmosphere that is characteristic of the Children's Bureau. The agency's multiple layers of civil servants and ubiquitous political appointees, many who are inexperienced and disinterested in the child welfare field and in management, make strategic planning difficult, if not impossible, if the issues are not clearly defined administration priorities. For the few intrepid internal advocates, promoting substantive new programs within and outside the agency is a Sisyphean effort requiring great patience. The competitive grant process made it difficult, but not impossible, to plan and carry out the strategic placement of funds. Bureau personnel made their preferences known to reviewers in the competitive proposal review process. Furthermore, the funding objectives were clear in the wording of the discretionary grant announcements to the experienced applicant.

A review of fifteen years of memoranda between program officers and their supervisors and chiefs in the Children's Bureau reveal common threads of frustration and despair. Limits on the number of grants, restrictions placed on applicants, and the small dollar amount of awards, undoubtedly increased the number of organizations that self-selected out of the competition. In contrast, the Clark foundation sought out programs that were prepared to adopt the family preservation Homebuilders model, and was strategic in its choice of grantees.

A Clark grantee became part of a larger network of family preservation programs that included training and support from members of the original Homebuilders program, other grantees, and the foundation staff. Although some objected to the regimentation, Clark grantees appeared, at least initially, to be happy with the program. Foundation representatives freely admit to problems in maintaining the integrity of the Homebuilders program model; grantees made adaptations that facilitated their work in their communities. Nevertheless, contrasted with the foundation's plan for promoting family preservation, the Children's Bureau efforts were barely visible.

Even the well-orchestrated strategic efforts of the Clark foundation were no match for the child welfare system. Although Clark's grantees were private agencies (grants to public agencies were used to contract with private agencies) each required the cooperation of, and referrals from, public agencies and the courts. To make the best use of the trained professionals in the family preservation program, the families referred should be those who: 1) exhibited dysfunctional behaviors that might result in removal of a child, and 2) had some hope of rehabilitation during the program's short-term, service-intensive time frame. And, this is the rub. To make such referrals, public agency caseworkers must be able to assess a family's circumstances, making a determination as to whether referral to a family preservation service is indicated.

As noted earlier, the diagnostic skills of poorly trained caseworkers may not be up to the task. Furthermore, faced with the alternatives of placement or family preservation, family court judges are likely to order referrals that cannot be countermanded by the family preservation staff. If family preservation services are ill used, they become too expensive. Expending intensive services on families that cannot be rehabilitated, or families that are able to function with the aid of counseling and material services is wasteful; however, rational public agency workers will be inclined to refer the former, and rational family preservation workers will be inclined to accept the latter. These are common problems for categorically defined family preservation services, and common frustrations for family preservation advocates.

In the meantime, the people at the Children's Bureau-funded National Resource Center on Family Based Services were discovering similar problems in the agencies with which they were working. Saddled with the Reagan administration appointees' *dicta* 'to earn their keep', the center staff seemed to be losing ground in advocating for family based services. Unlike the Clark foundation grantees that worked principally with private agencies, the resource center worked with public agencies. Although the center was successful in selling written materials produced by the staff, and in contracting for worker training, it was obvious that unless agencies were able to re-structure themselves to control the size of their caseloads, training in family-based techniques would simply frustrate public agency workers.

The techniques being taught could be used with most families amenable to counseling; however, high caseloads often prevented caseworkers from applying their new skills. Caseloads were only part of the problem. The Clark foundation strategy included educating other community stakeholders about the advantages of adopting a family preservation approach. This was more difficult for the resource center staff members who, because of their dependence on training contracts with public agencies, had fewer opportunities to affect the attitudes of others in the service community. These elements, namely the courts and other service providers, often worked at cross-purposes with the public child welfare agency in the latter's efforts to adopt a family practice approach to casework. The contentiousness of community stakeholders may have been due to a well-earned distrust of the competence of public agency workers. It may also have been due to internecine jealousies and the unwarranted concern that public agency workers trained as therapists might result in fewer contracts with private community service providers.

## Conclusion

Theories on policy formation more often than not presume some rational order to the process that, when followed, yields 'good' policy, although their authors concede that the process is 'messy' consequent on the complexity of the problem involved (See Dunn 1993). One of the first elements in the process is a demonstrable need, or social problem. Steadily increasing foster care placements and the length of time children were spending in foster care satisfied the demonstrated need for an alternative policy for handling family social service cases in which a child's placement was a real possibility. The pressure from advocates, and the drain on the resources of state and local child welfare agencies, despite unlimited federal matching funds, make alternatives to foster care attractive. Family preservation was such an alternative.

A second element is a policy alternative that is sufficiently compelling to make changing current policy worthwhile. Family based practice had been suggested as an alternative to out-of-home placement as early as the 1940s. All that was needed to make it the preferred approach, was a program that had demonstrated success over time, was easily understood by practitioners and lay-people (including policy makers), and that could be replicated repeatedly under diverse circumstances. The Homebuilders program satisfied these qualifications. It had been in operation for at least ten years, had demonstrated the utility of its approach in maintaining intact families, albeit families whose children were adolescents involved in the juvenile justice system.

Homebuilders had documented a treatment approach that was reasonably easy to describe, even to lay persons, and, although a private agency, it had established a positive working relationship with the state agency with which it was contracting for service referrals. It was also fully professionalized: its treatment staff were credentialed, master's level professionals who were competently supervised. And importantly, its executives were willing and deferential participants in the plan to 'go public' under the sheltering wing of the Clark Foundation's professional staff and its generous grants. The policy marketing approach worked—up to a point. It was possible to package the Homebuilder's product and market it successfully to program developers and policy makers, nation-wide. However, after the start-up grants ceased and continuation funding dried up, the programs funded by the Clark Foundation gradually began dropping away, altering their programs into barely recognizable semblances of the original Homebuilder's model.

The contrasts between the two groups, the family based practitioners and the family preservationists (Homebuilder-type) can be viewed as a metaphor for many of the problems that plague the country's child welfare system. There is the 'can't see the forest for the trees' focus on micro-level issues on the one hand, and on the other hand, the 'one size fits all' blindness to the breadth, depth, and complexity of the human circumstances for which social services to date have been so poorly designed. The family preservationists exhibited a single-minded, almost cult-like devotion to maintaining the purity of their program, discounting all others, while over-selling its importance as an antidote to foster care. This is contrasted with the family based practitioners who demonstrated an equal devotion to their systemic, or ecologically-oriented collection of treatment methods but who were politically naïve about, or generally disinterested in the larger systemic issues or macro-level policies that determine the nature of the child welfare system. They showed a general disinterest in evaluating their programs, were less likely to describe their program in replicable terms and in fact, in many instances, had difficulty articulating exactly what it was that they were doing with families.

The policy change process also requires political will. Demonstrable need and feasibility are not sufficient for effecting changes in social policy if political support is absent; however, garnering political support for social programs generally requires some evidence of both. The evidence doesn't necessarily need to be empirical; family preservation policy is a case in point. As we will discuss in the next chapter, very few research studies have supported the efficacy of family preservation as a method for the prevention of foster care placement. Yet policies were made on this basis alone with the promise that new funding was unnecessary since family preservation could be paid for with foster care savings. Most observers familiar with the child welfare system know well that, unless placement options are moderated, out of home placement will be used by overburdened workers with little time to think through alternative options. It is axiomatic: if a bed is available, it will be used.

To suggest that a program alternative will substitute for placement is naïve. A more realistic objective might include reduced caseloads—also a stated objective of family preservation. Unfortunately, the focus of caseload reductions has been limited to a few service units in the agency, or to a contracted service provider, leaving other units and other service providers free to use available foster care resources (and to resent the special privileges of the family preservation workers). Of course, caseload reduction alone cannot stanch the flow into foster care. As we discussed in Chapter 3, and will again address in our final chapter, the complex problems that bring families to the attention of child welfare agencies require thinking beyond the box.

An apparently effective marketing device is describing a concept in a simple, easily remembered phrase—Just Say No! Three Strikes You're

Out! Family Preservation. However, such devices are only temporarily useful, masking the complexity of the problems they proposed to remedy. When implementation reveals weaknesses, as it inevitably does, the program's detractors are presented with the ammunition they need for declaring the program a failure and the program's advocates find themselves in a defensive, back-pedaling mode. An offensive position—proposing a new program designed to solve a very difficult, and lingering problem—dissolves into a defensive position. In child welfare, the new program joins a long list of failed efforts. The hope is that it will be rehabilitated at a later date, revised and improved by some future group of advocates.

Family preservation has not exhibited a death rattle as yet; however, it's principal advocates have backed away from their earlier claims for success and acknowledged their mistake in not doing a more thorough evaluation of program outcomes prior to giving family preservation their unequivocal backing.[7] Nonetheless, the fact that family preservation and its counterparts among the family systems practitioners have become a part of the child welfare system—in name if not in practice— is due, in our view, in large part to the remarkable strategic work of the Clark foundation and those program operatives that it funded for the better part of a decade. If left to the plodding efforts of the Children's Bureau, family preservation and family based practice would probably be little more than a footnote in the history of the bureau's recent work

Whether or not the family practice advocates will be successful in their efforts to redirect the focus from the child to the family remains to be seen. Peter Forsythe resigned from his position at the Clark Foundation, replaced by Susan Notkin, who maintains that the Foundation is still a committed advocate of family preservation services despite having redirected its social action commitment elsewhere.[8] Although family preservation is not a household word, it is recognized, if not implemented, in public child welfare agencies. There is no question in our minds that the Clark Foundation was instrumental in the process that led to this event. The National Association for Family-Based Services' thirteenth annual empowering families conference program (1999) had as its theme, community partnerships, suggesting that the organization recognized the advocacy power that embracing the multiple discourses of the larger service community can afford (see Wattenberg and Pearson 1997).

## NOTES

[1]Sponsored by the Lower East Side Family Union settlement house, the multidisciplinary case-planning program became a model emulated by many other child welfare organizations.

[2]Interview with Susan Notkin, Director of Children's Programs, Edna McConnell Clark Foundation, November 2, 1999.

[3] Littner, 1956; Maas and Engler, 1959; Geiser, 1973; Knitzer and Allen, 1978; Persico, 1979.

[4] Parent education usually involves sending a client to parenting classes where "parenting" is taught, often without the child present. Modeling parenting involves working side-by-side with a parent and child in the home, much as a grandmother might demonstrate for her daughter how to diaper her grandchild.

[5] Very briefly, the systems or ecological approach views the family as a system that "operates" within and among other systems including the community, school, job, and that each has an impact to a greater or lesser degree on family functioning.

[6] The Child Welfare Resource Information Exchange, described earlier, identified several of the same family based treatment programs almost ten years earlier; however, no action was taken by the Children's Bureau to promote them after the Information Exchange contract was not renewed.

[7] Interview with Susan Notkin, Director of Children's Programs, Edna McConnell Clark Foundation, November 2, 1999.

[8] Notkin interview, November 2, 1999.

# Chapter 6

## Studies of Child Welfare and Family-Based Practice

*Introduction*

Defining the characteristics of family-based practice becomes problematic when the desire to package services in some pre-determined manner results in privileging one set of characteristics over another (Whittaker 1990). For example, family preservation advocates have differentiated program services by venue (in-home or in-office), orientation in time (short- mid- and long-term), the size of the caseload, the degree of flexibility and autonomy that workers are given, and whether they are solely therapeutic or some blend of concrete and therapeutic services. It would seem that our search for the grand design—the program that solves the problem—when the problems are multiple, is at heart, the issue.

We have repeatedly suggested that in 'packaging' a program or service, as the Clark Foundation did with the Homebuilder's program, we privilege it and marginalize all of the others. As the studies of family preservation services in the 1990s demonstrated, the fixation on prevention of foster care as a successful outcome and the failure of these studies to show a relationship between these services and preven-tion of placement, gave those who doubted their usefulness the opportunity to discredit and further marginalize these programs. Some evaluators have responded by searching for better statistics, for example, hazard rate analysis (Whittaker 1990, 8, citing Fraser, Pecora, & Hapaala), others look to multimethod research designs, and still others seek experimental methods using randomly selected national samples with experimental and control groups (Rossi 1992b). Defining successful outcomes is not a research problem—it is a programmatic one. It is the researcher's task to help program staff articulate these outcomes in researchable terms. As Whittaker (1990) remonstrates, "Let us not shy from objectives that are difficult to measure, simply because they are difficult, particularly when they reflect a fundamentally human aspiration or expression (12)."

Over the past century, the uses for evaluation research have grown in conjunction with the emphasis on social science research, and the desire among all three branches of the federal government and state governments for information on the relative worth of programs supported by public funds. However, in the impoverished field of child welfare where new programs are grudgingly supported in federal and state budgets, evaluation research is often haphazard, poorly financed, and viewed as an impediment by program managers rather than a source of information for planning and assessing program claims. In this chapter, we review some of the methodological issues that researchers have been grappling with in child welfare studies and family based practice evaluations in their efforts to craft and conduct sound research studies. We conclude that the under-funding, endemic to virtually every element of child welfare, plagues efforts to understand the truth of outcome claims by program developers, as well. This, along with issues in operationalizing therapeutic interventions and therapist skills variables, present challenges to the most experienced and creative researchers.

## Federal Response to Evaluation

Researchers experienced in conducting studies in child welfare in public agencies and the private agencies that contract with them, are familiar with the problems associated with designing studies, collecting data and reporting findings that can withstand the critical review of their peers. Although each study site poses interesting issues that are unique to its operating environment, there are also difficulties that can be cited as common across the field. For example, states have been slow to computerize their social service programs and many have experienced difficulties developing computerized information systems that systematically collect data useful for short- and long-range decision-making, and for evaluating service outcomes. There are at least four contributing factors to the states' tardiness in this area: 1) difficulties in conceptualizing aspects of casework in meaningful, quantifiable formats, 2) the resistance of caseworkers to using systems that do not give them a return on time invested in entering information, 3) a paucity of funds for developing and maintaining both hardware and software, and 4) contractors that exaggerate their capacity to design and implement the software product. The speed with which technology is advancing and the glacial slowness with which procurement systems operate often render computer systems obsolete before installation is complete.

A general lack of reliable case information compounds difficulties in conducting methodologically sound quantitative research studies. Collecting data directly from written case records is extremely time-consuming and therefore, costly. Although this method may still be the best one for assessing the nature and extent of the services provided, the thoroughness of written case files are inconsistent even within the same agency. Comparisons among similar programs in different agencies are beset with inconsistencies in the terminology used to describe clients and their problems and the services provided. Methods of defining and thereby counting clients are also problematic. Who is the client: the mother or the identified child among a family of children who may also benefit from services, or the family as a whole?

Child welfare evaluation studies are a research minefield. Nevertheless, we concur with Newcomer, Hatry and Wholey (1994) that, "It is better to be roughly right than precisely ignorant (1)." Evaluation is a necessity, particularly in a field as fraught with problems as are child welfare services in the United States. Although interest has grown in conducting qualitative studies, this branch of social science research has found acceptance to be slow going among the dominant group of classically trained researchers. The case study approach, in which a single agency or program is thoroughly examined, can enlighten, but be of questionable utility in making comparisons across programs and sites.

Unlike other public services that have broader, more politically active constituencies—public health, education, law enforcement—social services, including child welfare, generate little public interest, and attract few professional researchers who can claim sophisticated skills in statistical analysis, and even less funding for substantial research (the latter generally draws the former). A recent exception has been studies on welfare reform, adopted as a pivotal political issue between Republicans and Democrats in the continuing debate over excesses in government spending. Most of the state studies began when reforms in the welfare system required federal waivers and before legislation authorized the changes that made these waivers unnecessary. Research is costly (but not as costly as errors that result from policies made without benefit of empirical data), and takes longer to complete than many policy makers are willing to wait. Furthermore, studies often yield unsatisfying results—supporting the null hypothesis that no change has occurred and the need for further study.

It is also likely that research will point out a system's deficits and suggest the need for additional resources including money. Rather than adopting the long view that such findings provide a basis for altering a policy or program—inconclusive or negative findings are anathema to a program's advocates and ammunition for critics who wish to discredit an entire policy or program. It is little wonder that program evaluation is viewed with skepticism, even dread by program advocates. A study's findings reported in abstruse language befuddle the untrained reader, suggesting that both researchers and practitioners need to find common ground. Nevertheless, when research is reported and links are found between the research source and its potential users, findings are eagerly shared among practitioners. The intensity of the field's thirst for information is so strong that research findings are often accepted as truth despite the conceptual and methodological flaws that are evident to a study's authors and their colleagues (Rossi 1992a, 1992b; Littell and Schuerman 1994; Epstein 1998).

The language of research is associated principally with academic disciplines. In the social sciences, researchers are usually able to communicate across their respective fields; however, research discourse is considered arcane by most policy makers and practitioners, even among those in the same discipline. This problem, the interpretation and use of research, has been studied under the rubric 'knowledge use' or 'knowledge utilization.' Most of the research studies in knowledge use were done over a 30-year period beginning in the early 1960s. Among the questions that knowledge use scholars sought to answer were whether and how scholarly research was actually used by practitioners in the field. The early literature involving knowledge use focuses on problems related to the flow of information between knowledge producers (researchers) and knowledge users (practitioners) with various models proposed to facilitate interactions among them. Although results were mixed, knowledge produced by professional and academic researchers was generally linked to both conceptual and instrumental uses. Conceptual use has been defined as leading to changes in the way users think about problems; instrumental use occurs when knowledge results in behavioral changes (Weiss 1980, Hutchinson 1992).

A 1982 study conducted by Van de Vall and Bolas in the Netherlands examined the impact on policy of client-oriented social research in 3 policy-making sectors, one of which was social welfare. An important function of such research was found to be consensus-building which is related to inter-organizational dependence and a high rate of researcher-consumer interaction. The authors also confirmed, as others had before them, that publishing research findings in scholarly and professional journals correlated negatively with policy impact. Several later studies (Weiss 1980, Hutchinson 1995) suggest that research which is perceived to be of high quality, its academic derivation notwith-standing, is sought out and used by decision makers in the mental health and child welfare organizations surveyed.

The use of linking agents as interpreters of research findings, particularly when such agency occurs through person-to-person contacts, is preferred over reading scholarly journals. Linking agents may be individuals, for example, consultants, or events, as with professional conferences, workshops, or formal information and referral sources that produce newsletters, and the like. These same studies suggested that research has found its uses among policy makers and practitioners in the groups studied, contradicting the view held by those who have acted to systematically reduce funding for research, that research is of little practical value.

Nevertheless, the schism between academic researchers and in-the-field practitioners continues. In general, the distrust that practitioners share for academic research seems misplaced. In fact, it may have less to do with language deficits than with conflicting discourses where status and timing play a significant role. Practitioners want speedy answers that produce clear indicators as to the direction a program must take. On the other hand, academic researchers seek recognition among their peers by presenting findings at professional conferences and publishing research results in academic journals, a time consuming process. Also, program evaluations, the most common form of research in the field, are not likely to produce the scholarly recognition that academic researchers seek.

As was noted in Chapter 3, in its earlier days, the Children's Bureau played the role of both knowledge producer and knowledge disseminator. Its child welfare experts produced studies designed to inform policy decisions, and interpreted study findings to policy makers and practitioners in the field. However, following its dispersion in the 1960s, the bureau's funds were redirected to new program initiatives, called demonstrations, and away from research studies. Those who complained about this state of affairs were principally researchers, not practitioners. During the impressive push for new social programs for which billions of dollars were spent in the 1960s and 1970s, critics demanded proof that these new programs actually worked, and it became common practice to include an evaluation requirement in requests for proposals for federal grants and contracts.

In writing the forward to Suchman's book *Evaluative Research* (1967), Cottrell describes what he calls the ritualistic inclusion of an evaluation section in federal funding proposals. In some cases, these evaluation sections are grandiose but vague statements of intent and procedure. In other cases they are highly academic but impractical schemes developed by researchers. Cottrell observes that, "In a few treasured instances there is a well-considered, realistic, and workman-like plan for getting some fairly reliable answers to the questions of what worked and why (vii)."

Unfortunately, the evaluation mandate instituted by federal funding agencies offered little guidance to grantees on how such evaluations should be conducted. As a consequence, evaluations were only rarely taken seriously either by the grantee or the grantor. Funding allocations to agencies by congress for discretionary programs (the agency has the discretion to select the type of program to be funded) tended to be for grants that demonstrated methods for solving a particular social problem, noted with cynicism by some as the 'program *du jour*'. The motivating force behind this policy apparently has been that federal funds should not be used for on-going programs, but rather for innovative approaches to solving continuing social problems.

Once a program model had been funded, new submissions for funding similar programs were not considered innovations, and funding them was discouraged. The irony, of course, is obvious. Without substantive impact evaluations, it was not possible to determine whether or not an innovation had an effect on the social problem for which it was designed. This also means that the inter-subjectivity prized by researchers is subverted—the results of one evaluation cannot be compared with the results of other similar evaluations for the purpose of theory building. Furthermore, without the benefit of substantive evaluations, program developers had little to show for their efforts once federal funding ceased and it became necessary to seek local sources of support to continue their work. Although evaluation results were no guarantee of continued funding, the case for continuation was at least made stronger by its presence. Nevertheless, research, particularly program evaluations, were not a priority between 1979 and 1991, the years when family based practice was being touted as an alternative to foster care placement.

## Issues in Evaluation

Methodological rigor was and continues to be an issue among researchers in child welfare. Cottrell's observation, written in the 1960s, remains relevant today. Evaluations associated with federally funded projects are often unrealistic in their design by being either overly ambitious, or lacking in substance. Trying to do too much with too little is a problem for experienced and inexperienced researchers alike. Requiring research evaluation without sufficient funding to do it justice is the funding agency's error.

Funds notwithstanding, well-conceived, third-party evaluations may be subverted by the program's administrators and staff who, by refusing to cooperate, sabotage the evaluation process, or in their desire to see their claims substantiated, attempt to influence evaluation outcomes. Pressures on program administrators to prove program claims in order to secure additional year funding places evaluators in the awkward position of substantiating results when there is as yet insufficient information to support them. Concern that an external evaluator's loyalty is to the evaluation and not to the program (an entirely righteous position for an evaluator) may lead program personnel to withhold potentially damning information. They may record information incorrectly, or not record it at all. They may propose only clients who can articulate success for inclusion in the study, clients may be prepped for interviews, and agency personnel may purposely avoid contact with the evaluator.

Researchers who must depend upon caseworkers to collect information introduce expectancy bias, that is, consciously or unconsciously recording information that biases a program favorably— or unfavorably. When control groups are a part of the design, the occurrence of the 'John Henry' effect is a distinct possibility, that is, when competition arising between the workers serving clients in the control group leads to enhanced outcomes for the control group, thus confounding the research findings.

Neither are researchers necessarily above reproach. Fearing that their services will no longer be retained if the results that they produce are negative, research findings may be presented in equivocal language, and certain outcomes may be suppressed, although the latter has been more often a tactic of the funding agency. Prevarication or stonewalling of this sort, although ethically repugnant, can be, in our view, the result of unrealistic time constraints associated with demonstration funding—the need to fit programs into fiscal years—and of pressures inherent in the competition for scarce program and research money, or, in the matter of stonewalling, fear of political embarrassment. Finally, academic researchers are not often rewarded for conducting program evaluations, particularly if they cannot be seen to be contributing to some broader theoretical construct.

Despite the occasional manifestations of system-imposed impediments, research has produced some interesting and useful program-related information, discussed below. Although one may yearn for an unequivocal answer to the social problem a program is designed to remedy, this is rarely the case. Complex social problems can neither be solved with a single research project nor a single evaluation study. It is unfortunate indeed that researchers have been unable to adequately convey this basic research concept to policy makers who continue to make decisions based on inadequately supported claims, political considerations, anecdotal information, and blind faith.

## Studies of Child Welfare Services

A study conducted by Kamerman and Kahn (1989), looked at twenty-eight public and private child welfare agencies in an effort to assess the state of the art, as it were, of child welfare services at that time. The sites represented different types of service delivery: direct and indirect (purchased from private agencies), large urban agencies, and smaller agencies, and agencies in states that are state administered (workers in these states tend to be state employees) or state supervised (workers are local county or city employees that are indirectly supervised by the state). This was not a randomized sample and is not considered generalizable beyond the study's participants. Nevertheless, the conclusions reached by the researchers support the now ubiquitous complaints of difficulties experienced in child welfare agencies, including an almost single-minded focus on child abuse and neglect complaints to the exclusion of preventive services.

Kamerman and Kahn describe a number of deficiencies in the organizations they observed as well as an enormous increase in paperwork and compliance monitoring with associated burdens on staff, as a result of child welfare legislation. They also confirmed perceptions that large numbers of children of all ages with very serious problems were entering the child welfare system and community service network without the commensurate increases in financial and professional resources to meet their needs.

The authors cite a "dramatic increase in drug addiction, homelessness, AIDS, as well as the growing numbers of deinstitutionalized or not-institutionalized young developmentally disabled and mentally ill [children], some of whom also become parents themselves" (Kamerman and Kahn 1989, iv-v). Furthermore, we share the researchers' concerns "for the sometimes inconsistent, often unclear, and inappropriate interventions of some courts [that] create additional problems for staff and administrators in the social services" (v). A decade has passed since this research was reported, yet little has changed.

The Administration for Children and Families (DHHS) funded two national studies, one published in 1977 (Shyne and Schroeder 1980), and another published in 1994 (Department of Health and Human Services), both of which provide broad-brush pictures of the state of child welfare services in the periods immediately preceding their publication. Both confirm the difficulties faced by local and state agencies in meeting their obligations to their clients. Because of their national scope and the difficulties in comparing services across states, both studies suffer from a lack of specificity where detail would be most helpful for program developers.

The comparisons between the two studies show a troubling lack of progress in child welfare services, generally, over the twenty years between data collection periods. The so-called foster care drift noted in the earlier study had not abated despite provisions in the Adoption Opportunities and Child Welfare Act of 1980 (Public Law 96-272) requiring six-month administrative and dispositional hearings for children in foster care. It is noted in the later study, that over one-third of children in foster care remain longer than eighteen months, although the overall length of time in care decreased, on average. Furthermore, in the 1994 study, African-American and Hispanic children were found to be twice as likely to be placed in foster care as white children.

The authors compared the circumstances of children across races, that is, their general characteristics and presenting problems, to determine whether race was a factor. They found that after controlling for such circumstances as employment, neighborhood crime and drug usage, caretaker substance abuse, and physical and mental disabilities, and the number of presenting problems, African-American children were still more likely to be placed in foster care than their white counterparts (1994 Study xii-xiii). This very disturbing finding is not a new one, with similar disparities reported in much earlier studies (Jeter 1963; Fanshel 1978). The 1994 Children's Bureau study also pointed out that, since the study reported in 1977, in-home, family-based services had become commonplace. However, in comparison to foster care services, family-based services were offered to only a small fraction of child welfare clients. For example, the Homebuilders program in Washington State served approximately fifty children a month while, at the same time, 500 children were placed in foster care.

Caseloads reported by counties show a similar relation. For instance, in 1994, 78 families received family preservation services in Contra Costa, California while the comparable number of foster care cases that were opened totaled 589 in 1994. During this same time period in Suffolk county, New York, 100 families received family preservation services while 453 entered foster care. (DHHS National Study 1994, 1-15)

## Placement Prevention Studies

The placement prevention requirements of the Adoption Opportunities and Child Welfare Act of 1980 (Public Law 96-272) did not become effective until October 1, 1983, at which time states were required to certify in an administrative review that they had a program. At the same time, judges reviewing foster care placements were required to specify that 'reasonable efforts' had been made to prevent the need for placement before the cost of a child's foster care could be reimbursed to the state under the Social Security Act Title IV-E foster care provisions. The act did not require that states have prevention programs until the $256 million authorization for child welfare services (Title IV-B) was reached, and additional funds were not provided over and above this amount, although in some circumstances, Title IV-E money could be transferred.

A 1983 Survey of Prevention and Reunification Programs by Portland State University indicated that in all fifty-one states, prevention was an agency goal. Thirty listed reunification after placement as a specific goal. Thirty-six had developed guidelines for prevention services, and twenty-eight, for reunification; however, only twenty-six states required a written case plan. Services for preventing foster care were not uniformly available; the most common reasons for their scarcity were a lack of resources and funding. Federal figures on the number of children in foster care between 1977, when the first National Study (Shyne and Schroeder 1977) was reported, and 1983, when the Portland study was released, showed a 47 percent decrease, from 502,000 in 1977, to 263,992 children in 1983. At the same time, child abuse and neglect reports increased 43 percent from 838,000 in 1977, to 1,477,000 in 1983. (In 2001, there were an estimated 2,934,000 reports[1].)

An internal Children's Bureau report (Sudia 1985) attributes the dramatic decrease in foster care placements to a national dissemination program on permanency planning conducted by the Children's Bureau between 1977 and 1980. As a result of the attention, many states turned their long-term foster care placements into adoptive placements, returned children to their original families, and reconstituted 'temporary' placements into permanent foster care placements. Other foster children simply aged out of the system. However, the increase in abuse and neglect reports was having an affect on foster care placements, which by 1984 was signaling an upward trend. This increase continued with a leveling off in the 1990s at upwards of half a million children in care at any given time.

The same report cites a study by the Department of Health and Human Services on the use of emergency placements in three states. The study suggested that greater use of emergency foster care was caused by state policy, the relationship of child welfare services to the juvenile justice and mental health systems, and the lack of preventive services. For example, if a state accepted only the most urgent cases, emergency placements were greater and fewer prevention services were offered. Some child welfare systems were responsible for placing youths from the juvenile justice system (status offenders and incipient delinquents). And, some child welfare agencies accepted voluntary relinquishments of children whose parents were unable to cope with them because of their own or their child's illness or incapacity, or because the child was 'out of control.' The report suggests that despite the presence of these factors, counties in at least one state were able to control emergency placements by establishing a review system and preventive services.

The prevention strategies suggested in the Children's Bureau report were two-fold: 1) negotiating with the court to gain control over the agency's foster care placements with diversion of juveniles, developmentally disabled and emotionally ill children to more appropriate agencies; and 2) implementing diversion programs in child welfare. For abuse cases, rather than limiting services to the most severe, the report suggests that parent aides, parent education, day care, homemaker services, concrete services (such as buying a refrigerator, if needed) and parent counseling had proven effective methods for reducing out-of-home care. It warns that even systematic placement prevention programs may succeed only in maintaining the status quo, and that states without such programs are expected to see an increase in placement rates, a prophecy which was subsequently realized.[2]

## Family Based Evaluations

Family based practitioners have struggled to maintain the credibility of their programs in the face of evaluation findings that are far from conclusive, particularly as they relate to prevention of foster care placements. As was noted earlier in this work, prevention of foster care was the principal motivational tool used to market the types of intensive family-focused services that were later known as family preservation. Indeed, the term 'preservation' connotes preserving families from the disruptions of out-of-home placement. It is not our purpose to review these studies; this has been done. A summary of research conducted from the 1970s through 1995 is presented by Littell and Schuerman (May 1995), available on the Internet.

Rossi (1992), in a much more detailed critique of family preservation evaluations, does a particularly perceptive analysis of selection bias and the use of foster care placement as an outcome measure. What is clear from reading the authors' critiques of prior research, and is evident to other researchers reading study findings, is that few used controlled studies, and those that did use controls encountered numerous problems with maintaining the integrity of the research design over the course of the study period. Although these studies found little support for the claims that family preservation is succeeding as a method for preventing foster care placements, Rossi, in particular, points out design flaws that bring assertions regarding placements, positive or negative, into question. More recent studies also suggest that there is no significant difference in foster care prevention between family preservation cases and the more traditional cases in the control group

(James Bell Associates 1999, Westat *et al* 2001). The Westat study makes the claim that family preservation is not focused enough—apparently attempting to reinforce the notion of categorical specialization—a position we suggest is at the heart of the child welfare system's problems (17).

The earliest studies reviewed by Littell and Scheureman (1995) that examine in-home services were not family preservation studies *per se*, but were studies of families whose children were not in foster care. Child welfare agencies have historically provided some level of services to families in their own homes, most often counseling, concrete or hard services (e.g., emergency funds for beds, or baby equipment), parent education, homemaker services, and referral services to other agencies, among others. For example, we recall a story about one family whose chaotic circumstances subsided almost immediately when the caseworker removed an out-of-control dog. Sometimes it takes an outsider to see the obvious. Such services are quantifiable.

Family preservation services patterned after the Homebuilders and therapy-based models can be quantified by the number of personal contact hours with family members; however, the degree of change by any or all family members that result from these contacts is more difficult to assess, particularly in the long-term. If the change results in divorce, is that a positive or a negative outcome? Also difficult to assess are the quality of in-home therapeutic services. Measured against a family's circumstances at first contact with the agency, that is, the level of 'dysfunction', it may be possible to measure change. However, this pre-post measurement design requires at minimum, a base-line assessment of family functioning prior to beginning intensive therapeutic services, either in-home or in-office. As Rossi (1992) notes, such assessments are difficult to measure given the level of crisis the family may be experiencing, and the worker's level of expertise in the assessment process.

Various tools for assessing risk, that is, risk of harm to a family's children, and for assessing outcomes based on measures of family functioning have been devised. In fact, most states now have at least some type of risk assessment as a matter of practice. However, these tools presume a level of worker competence and commitment that may or may not be present in the work-a-day setting of the child welfare agency. Developers of the tools presume that workers have time to learn and use them. Since, as we noted in earlier chapters, many of the workers employed in public child welfare agencies receive their training on the job, their successful use of these tools depends on a supportive agency policy and competent supervision. Moreover, such tools must be internalized by the worker to be truly effective—visualize the alternative: a caseworker armed with clip board and pencil, checking off measures of family functioning while interviewing family members—not a confidence-inspiring picture. Unfortunately, we don't really have a good understanding of what family caseworkers know and don't know. Both public agencies and their private contract providers may hire 'off the street', so to speak. And, to be fair, the caseworkers hired appear to be doing what they're asked to do and more.

Perhaps one of the reasons that so few families are afforded therapeutic family-based services is that genuine therapeutic skills take time and effort to acquire. Broader adoption by state agencies of family-based, family preservation programs may be prompted by federal incentives[3] and state legislated mandates. If so, it is reasonable to expect that the original programs marketed by the Edna McConnell Clark Foundation, and the National Resource Center on Family Based Practice, among others, would undergo adaptation to fit into an agencies' pre-family-based operating scheme. However, the original program design also may be subverted by using minimally trained workers with higher caseloads than desirable to achieve model program claims. We have only anecdotal observations to support this view; however, we note that the evaluation studies which suggest that no change has occurred, do not generally assess worker competencies as therapists other than to observe that workers were trained in a particular model. There are exceptions including the Yuan (1990, ii) study mentioned below, which describes workers as licensed.

One group of evaluators describe staff qualifications for home-based services as having skills in a variety of treatment modalities plus an attitude of genuine concern, optimism, and respect for clients. "For example, nonjudgmental attitudes and the formation of close supportive relationships with families are emphasized . . . by many home based service agencies. Specifying which worker skills and attitudes are associated with effective treatment is difficult; but this information is essential for program replication (8)." And, essential for effective program evaluation, we might add.

In the early years of family based service adoption—the late 1970s through the 1980s—the focus was not on evaluation, in fact, generally little thought was given to this aspect of program implementation. As has been noted in previous chapters, the focus of these programs was on convincing administrators and policy makers that family based services could help family members resolve the problems that brought them to the attention of the child welfare agency. Once recognized for its marketing advantages, the foster care prevention claim and the promise of cost savings, like wild fire, became virtually unstoppable.

The more difficult to describe merits of intensive family treatment were, and still remain important challenges for the evaluator. In describing family and child outcomes in their evaluation report of in-home care demonstration projects, Yuan (1990) wrote the following:

> Many families were able to learn new ways to parent their children. On the average, families improved in terms of mental health care for their children, their ability to provide continuity of parenting, their acceptance and approval of their children, their ability to recognize their problems, and their motivation to solve problems. (iv)

Although the Yuan study did not find statistically significant differences in foster care placements, or foster care expenditures between treatment families and those in the control group, improvements such as those described above are, in our view, precisely what the child welfare agency should be striving to achieve.

The discontinuity between the desire for methodological rigor, as prescribed by some researchers (Rossi, 1992a & 1992b; Littell & Schuerman 1995) and the practical difficulties in designing and implementing controlled studies poses a quandary for child welfare researchers, the heated discussions over which have unnecessarily wounded some combatants. Some of the rancor among researchers parallels the battle lines drawn between advocates of the Homebuilders model and the family-based models; however, their disagreements more often have to do with methodological orthodoxy—a common occurrence among researchers in this and other disciplines.

As we noted above, the context of these studies poses inherent difficulties, not the least of which is funding insufficiencies. It was clear to researchers and the Children's Bureau early on that limited funding could be ameliorated, at least to some extent, by giving researchers opportunities to share information and brainstorm problems and solutions with one another. Meetings, under varying auspices, among researchers have been held periodically to good effect, and while practical difficulties remain, some of the animosities among researchers have dissipated in favor of a respectful collegiality.

Fraser (1991), a veteran family preservation researcher, suggests that the community of service providers must be brought into the research mix as valued participants. Based on his research team's experiences, Fraser prescribes the involvement of workers, administrators and clients at the onset of a research project. Their involvement should include participating in all of the basic research elements from identifying research questions, and developing conceptual frameworks, to reviewing the research design, the data collection instruments, and presenting research findings. He maintains that involving study site stakeholders in these fundamental research activities can prevent poorly defined treatments that are inconsistently delivered.

Bringing stakeholders into the process may increase the time required to complete a study; however, it is also likely that doing so will overcome many of the obstacles described earlier that can foil the researcher's design and cast doubt on the veracity of a study's findings. We concur with Fraser's view that "family preservation services and the profession can benefit more from dozens of small studies than from several large ones" (See also, Nelson and Landsman 1990, 170). Concentrating on smaller, well-conceived and more easily controlled studies has the marked advantage of overcoming cross-jurisdictional inconsistencies in language and practice, while respecting the uniqueness of individual programs and their contextual differences, leaving to future researchers, the task of meta-analyses. Also an advantage of smaller studies, both qualitative and quantitative, is the level of detail and the depth of description that can be used by program developers to reproduce programs in their own settings.

## Conclusion

Program evaluations in child welfare in general, and family based practice, in particular, have been inconsistently funded over the years. The result is that policy makers and practitioners have been forced to make decisions based on a small number of studies—only a few of which would pass the test for scientific rigor. Not unlike the rest of child welfare, funds have been so scarce for research that the competition for funding can be cutthroat, and those who win research money may find that they must compromise for fear of offending their funding source. Local programs rarely have money to hire researchers, generally do not have trained researchers on their staffs, and must rely on local university faculty and students to conduct studies for them. It is, of course, easier to make policy in an information vacuum—that is, without the data that create questions, and pose political dilemmas. However, with the futures of so many children in the balance, the failure to adequately fund evaluation research at the local and state levels is indeed unfortunate.

---

### Notes

[1] U.S. Department of Health and Human Services press release entitled HHS reports new child abuse and neglect statistics, 2 April 2001, http://www.os.dhhs.gov/news/press/2001press/20010402.html.

[2] Internal memorandum, Children's Bureau, Office of Human Development Services, DHHS, December 17, 1985. (unattributed).

[3] In the report, Family Preservation and Family Support (FP/FS) Services Implementation Study, Interim Report, Administration for Children and Families, US Dept. of Health and Human Services, January 1998, it is noted that the flexibility given to states and localities in implementation of the provisions of the 1993 Family Preservation and Family Support Act (title IV-B, subpart 2 of the Social Security Act) produced considerable variation in results, including wide variability in interpreting what constitutes preventive services, p i-ii.

# Chapter 7

## Imagining a Re-constructed Child Welfare System

*Introduction*

The purpose in writing this book has been to create a picture of the challenges we face, nationally, and in our respective communities in responding to the needs of abused and neglected children and by calling for a cross-disciplinary discourse dedicated to imagining a reconstructed child welfare system. We use the family preservation movement as an example: the decisions and events which influenced the development and spread of family preservation services in the United States are examined for the lessons learned during the twenty year history beginning in the early 1970s and continuing to the 1990s. In this concluding chapter, three of its relevant discourses are examined once again, social work, family therapy, and public administration, to explore how each can contribute to the imagining and re-constructing processes. Although examples are given, and suggestions made, the conflating of discourses can only fruitfully be accomplished when the 'speakers' are purposefully engaged with one another.

In previous chapters, the general functions and structure of the public child welfare agency were described, as were some of the problems that these agencies face at the service provider level. The claim is made that child welfare has been abandoned, orphaned by the social work profession despite its origin in the discipline's history. The family therapy and public administration fields have had a tangential relationship to child welfare despite their potential as contributors to the public child welfare discourse. The historical foundations for family centered services and its incarnation as a prevention of foster care program were briefly touched upon, noting that, although the family is not a new service paradigm, viewing families as the locus of an integrated service approach that uses techniques developed by family therapists is a recent phenomenon in the public child welfare agency.

Nurturing the nascent family preservation approach has been compromised by several factors. First among these is the bureaucratic hierarchy and rule-driven organizational culture in child welfare that leaves little room for innovation. The term 'empowerment', now a cliché, was frequently used to describe one of the main tenets of the family preservation approach yet in the context of family functioning, its essence is largely unachievable. This is because the child welfare system is inflexible, unmoving, and repressive. In its current state, it is not a system that can empower anyone, clients or the workers who are responsible for them.

Related is the system's difficulty in attracting and maintaining a staff of professional employees who are rewarded for developing their skills and for their commitment to becoming family advocates rather than family surrogates. Administrators and policy makers who are reticent or unwilling to create service environments that are user-driven—that is, shaped by the particular needs and circumstances of its clients, and to take the risks that imaginative management and casework require— are making a political statement that these children and their families are not worthy of our best efforts.

The role played by the Children's Bureau in developing family preservation programs and policies was also examined. Its agency played a validating role in formalizing acceptance of family preservation services thereby encouraging national child welfare organizations and other stakeholders to take up the cause (see Minkoff 1994). Unfortunately, its contributions in the early years of family preservation services were attenuated by repeated reorganizations, inexperienced political appointees placed in administrative positions, and presidential administrations that had little interest in supporting the social services, particularly child welfare which was considered a local responsibility. In filling the leadership void created by an increasingly distanced Children's Bureau, the Edna McConnell Clark Foundation chose to promote a particular family-centered model, named its initiative family preservation, and developed a social marketing strategy that engaged the child welfare community in a contentious and protracted debate over the merits of the family preservation concept, generally, as well as particular program models. It then withdrew its support coincident with research findings suggesting that the relationship between service intensity and foster care placement, a principal marketing claim, was at best, uncertain.

Many of the programs studied by researchers were immature and were as yet poor candidates for evaluation. Furthermore, the quest for outcome measures that could adequately capture the subtleties of family functioning in and out of crisis and the changes in behaviors that might have been influenced by therapeutic interventions and other services, has been illusive. In the press of time-limited studies with limited funding resources, and anxiety over proving the worth of these programs, evaluators and their sponsors were pressured to accept as subjects families that did not meet the imminent placement criterion and agencies that were not committed to the model program design.

These, along with other methodological weaknesses cited in reports of evaluation studies (Rossi 1993a, 1993b; Littell & Schuerman 1995) continue to be debated by the community of family preservation researchers, with only a few recognizing the potential for qualitative and mutlimethod research designs (Wells & Freer 1994). Qualitative designs, it is suggested, respect the differences and diversity of both program and participants (families, workers, organizations) and seek to understand the language and meaning of the context in which they operate. Opportunities for new research now depend upon sponsors who recognize that theory building is a process that depends on the intersubjectivity of multiple researchers, multiple studies, and research methods that are designed to capture the subtle differences among respondents and models. Whether such support will be forthcoming cannot be answered here. Typically, however, sponsors of child welfare programs are quick to abandon them in favor of new ones—the program *du jour*—particularly when initial studies fail to show remarkable results.

We also discussed the notion of 'boxism', that is, the view that we are each limited by our constructions of our environment, and that when the environment is an organization structured along bureaucratic lines, our worldview tends toward the myopic. New ways of organizing our work are needed, in particular the work of child welfare. In order to expand our worldview, we must recognize and incorporate opportunities for multiple discourses. Discourse, as a social construction of meaning, is ideology, and as such is exclusionary. Discursive mechanisms limit what statements can be made and shape what is considered to be worth knowing. Farmer (2000) explores the possibilities of discourse analysis by using as metaphor the rungs on a ladder up which we are invited to climb: the first rung is 'me', the second is 'they', the third is 'ours' and the fourth leads us out of Plato's cave[1].

Me refers to a set of overlapping discourses (discourses are interrelated) in which the unit of analysis is reductionist, for example, me, my, mine, and the focus is on issues related to the individual in context, for example, my discipline, my organization. For 'they' the unit of analysis is also reductionist, but the issues extend to a system-wide context and the problematics that context entails, for example, the broader issues debated in our field. 'Our', the third rung in Farmer's ladder, connotes joint possession and includes the overlapping discourses that become possible when the scope of discourse opens up beyond walls built around disciplines.

In our view, the issues of family fragility and our community's responses to it (to dissolve a family by placing its children elsewhere, to maintain families at a minimal level of functioning and hope for the best, or to energetically support a family to prevent its dissolution) become 'ours' when the walls of multiple disciplines including social work, family therapy, and public administration are opened to explore options together. The fourth rung, 'out of the cave' suggests a unit of analysis that is not reductionist, but rather is emancipatory, exchanging the unidimensional human for the multidimensional human.

In our example, we re-conceputalize the bad parent as the bio-socio-psycho-spiritual parent and family member (Farmer 2000, 67-68). We recognize that what one discipline privileges, another marginalizes; but we also recognize that unity of disciplines is unlikely and probably even undesirable. What is possible is entertaining multiple perspectives and 'limited integrations (80).' In our earlier discussion of 'seriality' we suggest that the multiple, diverse associations that configure our relations with one another, once recognized, free us to move beyond 'walls'. We may be social workers, family therapists, family and child advocates, researchers, and administrators, and in recognizing that we are all of these, we open up the possibilities for artful imagining.

## Deconstructing Child Welfare

The dominant discourse of child welfare is child saving. However, the term child welfare could be construed to include the welfare of the child's family—the parent or parents and siblings in the conventional sense, or the custodian(s) with whom the child has a familial relationship, and beyond this, the welfare of the broader community. The state's involvement in the welfare of children has multiple dimensions, the most obvious being public education, public health, and indirectly, through employment opportunities, limited public financial aid, and aid-in-kind for adult family members. More recently, since the early 1970s, the state has defined and delimited parental behavior through legal prohibitions against various forms of child maltreatment.

The state also acts as surrogate when parents voluntarily relinquish their rights because they are financially, emotionally, or physically unable to care for a child.[2] The latter circumstance is of long standing, and was one of the foundational arguments for institutional care; they were once called orphanages, which some have proposed should be reinvented as an antidote to the shortage of foster family homes endemic to urban child welfare systems (See Thomas 1994). For better or worse, the recent history of child welfare remains one of child saving but with a new urgency since the advent of child abuse and neglect legislation.

Debate among professionals and child welfare advocates is remarkable for its constancy: the core system remains essentially the same while around it swirls controversy over which grand new plan will solve its problems. It would seem incumbent upon those who have made careers in the child welfare field to reconsider the state of child welfare in our communities and in the United States, to expand the discourse—to become inclusive, not exclusive. It is also incumbent upon those in other fields—fields that touch on the welfare of children—to demand to be included in the redesign of the child welfare system.

As Minuchin noted we have a tendency to operationalize only small parts of a problem without taking responsibility for the effect that such partializing has on other aspects of child welfare policy and the people these policies affect. For example, la turret offers a safe and anonymous option for abandoning a child; however, this solution does not deal with the broader issues of why children are abandoned. Foster care acts on the immediate problem of child abuse but does not acknowledge the larger issues of abusive behaviors, their causes and remedies.

Family preservation programs use therapeutic interventions while helping families meet their basic needs, thus combining the tasks of therapist and caseworker. However, as we have noted, these programs are a small, relatively insignificant part of the larger system. Advocates for abused children can be forgiven for attacking these prevention services (see Gelles 1993; Berliner 1993) given the history of failed programs in child welfare; however, as critics they are clearly in danger of throwing the baby out with the bath water. Their protestations reinforce those who would operationalize the role of child welfare as policing family dysfunction, removing children and giving them to someone else to rear. In so doing, there is the presumption that the problem is solved and that first, there is a sufficiency of foster families so charitably inclined; and, secondly, in these families or institutions a child's safety can be guaranteed.

Pelton (1990) takes a different view, suggesting that the police are the more appropriate institution to conduct child abuse investigations because they can better prosecute the offenders. (In fact, in the state of Florida, the sheriff's department is doing just this.)[3] Pelton proposes that a redefinition of the public child welfare response is in order since the agency's role in most jurisdictions has devolved to that of investigation and placement. He proposes that the agency's role be redefined as helper rather than investigator; however, in order to accomplish this, laws pertaining to child abuse must be significantly narrowed to exclude social neglect, by far the larger proportion of child protection complaints (Pelton 1990, 25).

Whether or not Pelton's proposal has merit is not the point. The claims made by Berliner and Gelles, along with Pelton's proposal are both reductionist. They are both second rung 'your' responses that define issues within the constructs of disciplinary walls (child saving with Berliner and Gelles, and prosecution vs. helping with Pelton). If child welfare is to be re-imagined and re-constructed, we must be open to different and diverse voices at the same time that we interrogate commonly held assumptions. The child saving voice marginalizes family-centered possibilities; Pelton's prosecution/helping dichotomy assumes that prosecution and helping are binary relations, when in reality the subjects of these relations are far more complex. One must be sympathetic to the frustrations with the child welfare system that lead to 'either/or' solutions; however, the multiple constructs that occupy the space in between call for multiple responses. The possibilities when thinking beyond the box, beyond the walls and categories that we devise are limited only by our imaginations.

Next we examine the possibilities for each of the principal discourses addressed in this book--social work, family therapy, and public administration--and then suggest a reconstruction of the role of federal and state governments in the matter of family and child services.

## Social Work

Four hypotheses were suggested by Hartman and Laird (1983, 12) to explain the uneasy relationship that existed between the nascent social work profession and the family: 1) the focus on the individual prompted by the mental hygiene/psychoanalysis/psychology move-ments; 2) the so-called 'inner' (individual) and 'outer' (social order) dichotomies; 3) limitations in the knowledge and theory base in social case work which made the integration of family into the psychological focus difficult if not impossible; and, 4) organizational arrangements of social work practice by method and field making it difficult to find a place for 'family'. This is not to say that the family was not acknowledged in social work's early years, nor is it an ignored element in theory and practice today; however, the family's encompassing characteristics defy specification within pre-existing categories.

We have made the claim that the social work profession has orphaned child welfare, and if the hypotheses posed by Hartman and Laird are correct, the field appears to have orphaned the family as well. Unlike other social work specializations, for example, mental health and health care that are both associated with the medical profession, and court services which are associated with the legal profession, child welfare has no close associations with other, more respected fields.

Although we recognize that academically trained, bachelor's and master's degree level social workers are present in line, supervisory, and administrative roles in the public child welfare agency, their number, according to the National Association of Social Workers (NASW), appears to be dwindling (see Chapter 1, EN 7). This event has led the NASW membership to request that the term 'social worker' not be used in reference to child welfare caseworkers, perhaps an admission of defeat, or possibly professional arrogance. If the profession's leadership is conceding defeat to policy makers who have systematically reduced the qualifications of employees filling casework positions in public child welfare agencies, we suggest that capitulation is premature. Their leadership is as important now as it was when the fledgling field was led by Jane Addams, Mary Richmond, and Edith Abbott,[4] among others.

We suggest that the social work profession, being now firmly established, may well look to other professions, other fields, to expand its knowledge base, and its capacities to respond to issues of public policy. Decrying the exclusion, "with differing degrees of rigidity to outside knowledge," Leonard (1994, 24) suggests that the "task of a critical social work practice and education might be seen as the search for alternative sources of knowledge . . . ." The sources that Leonard proposes are those that have been subordinated by the social mechanisms of class, gender and ethnic domination, as well as those that have flourished outside the discourses of objective, scientific knowledge, including literature, folklore and myth. As keepers of the archives of child welfare and family services knowledge, leadership is needed among social work practitioners and academics in re-constructing a child welfare that appreciates difference, diversity, and alternative discourses. Opening to alternative discourses suggests discursive communities facilitated by bridge-makers like Ann Hartman, for example, who has begun a bridging of discourses between social work and family therapy to the advantage of both.

We have suggested that professionalism in social work has contributed to the orphaning of child welfare. In his deconstruction of professionalism, Leonard (1995) is reminded of Foucault's argument that "professional power in the so-called 'caring professions' is essentially used for surveillance and control" (14-15). Lubove (1965, 161) points out that professionalism and bureaucracy are linked, and both, according to Leonard (1995) are a modernist phenomenon. Leonard argues that professionalism "privileges certain kinds of knowledge and expertise obtained through socialization within professional schools; its authority is locked into the class, gender, and ethnic structures of domination and legitimated by claims of technical effectiveness based upon the use of scientific 'advances' and the maintenance of normative order" (Leonard 1995, 15). He further argues for its re-construction on the order of Gramsci's (1971) 'organic intellectuals' that eschews elitism and incorporates a renewed interest in the demands for economic and social justice among the populations that social workers have historically served. In our view, the potentially emancipatory effects of dialogizing professionalism in social work (and the other helping fields) go hand in hand with establishing discursive communities. In imagining a re-constructed child welfare, both would have a salutary effect.

A re-constructed child welfare system should be open to new, radical ideas, as well as to old, discarded ones. The use of homemakers is an example of the latter. A study conducted by Mary Ann Jones (1976) found that workers in the experimental group who carried small caseloads and had access to a full range of concrete services, including homemakers and day care, experienced fewer foster care placements and witnessed a marked improvement in family functioning compared with the workers and families in the control group. Homemakers, like foster families, are not considered 'professionals', as the term is commonly defined; theirs is largely a housekeeping function with responsibilities for temporary parenting and the domestic tasks that that implies. The homemaker's role is relatively benign in that her power in relation to family members is minimal. She does not have the power to remove children nor to force behaviors although she can inform those who can. Homemaker services were popular in the 1950s and 1960s, but were largely abandoned by child welfare after that time, and are now used principally in programs for the aging. We may wish to re-think this decision.

## Family Therapy

Family therapy is a relatively recent sub-field in mental health. Its brief history is marked by the contributions of a diverse group of theorists and practitioners who were open to new possibilities, coming as they did from many different disciplines. Although the quest for an essential theory of family functioning is evident in the family therapy literature—a theory like the cybernetic-systems model, for example (Larner 1994)—in practice, family therapists are eclectic in their choice of therapies (quoting Goding, 12f). This quest has extended to the use of therapies in child welfare that includes the cognitive-behaviorists (exemplified by the Home-builder's program) that are not, strictly speaking, family therapists. Were it not for the political-ideological arguments that began with the involvement of the Clark Foundation, it is likely that the cybernetic-systems therapists and the cognitive-behaviorists and learning theorists would have coexisted, indeed, shared their strategies for working with families, with one another much earlier in the evolution of family preservation services. Friedman (1993) notes that "the competition over approach has infused clinical discussions with a political-ideological tension" that has led to a reifying of theory and to reductionism, both of which have resulted in an unnecessary confusion that is reflected in the thinking and behavior of family-centered practitioners (7-8).

This confusion, we suggest, has contributed to the marginalizing of family therapies in child welfare, as well. In our imagining child welfare, both family therapy and other interventions can coexist, as mutliple therapies can coexist. Larner (1994) has proposed a paramodern family therapy that plays on what he describes as the modern/postmodern dichotomy, using the construction 'both/and' as the preference over 'either/or,' an example noted in Friedman (1993, 7) being the use of multiple strategies to create an eclectic approach.

Child psychiatrist and family therapist, Salvador Minuchin (1967, 1998), has demonstrated repeatedly that treating families in the child welfare system is not only feasible, it is practical. In years of practice with poor families in poor neighborhoods, he demonstrated the utility of therapeutic techniques with very troubled families. Following Minuchin's example, therapists might test their mettle with families outside the practice realm of private family therapy much as free clinics depended on volunteer medical practitioners.

Therapists were employed as case consultants using a small federal grant ($60,000) in the Children and Youth Services Agency, Allegheny County (Pittsburgh), Pennsylvania with interesting results.[5] Therapists were assigned to units of caseworkers, who were encouraged to consult the therapist for techniques and advice in working with families. They were also encouraged to consult the therapists in dealing with their own personal problems and their frustrations with work. Therapists demonstrated their craft with families while seeing a side of family therapy not commonly found in the consulting room. Caseworkers observed and learned family therapy techniques following Gramsci's notion of organic collaboration (noted above and in Chapter 3, 63). Nevertheless, the agency chose not to continue the program with its own funds after the twelve month federal grant expired, citing as the reason, the ubiquitous budget shortfall. Caseworkers were slow to avail themselves of the therapists' time, and the program was not considered to be a priority. To its credit, the American Family Therapy Academy (AFTA) has been exploring the uses of family therapy with families in the child welfare system for over a decade now.

## Public Administration

The practitioners and theorists of public administration have the potential to make valuable contributions to the restructuring of child welfare. However, before this can occur there must be a compelling need, a motivating force that captures the attention and imagination of public administration thinkers. As with the field of social work, public administration could benefit from an examination of the boundaries and dimensions that define its areas of interest, and grow beyond these limitations. Indeed there is a growing contingent of public administration theorists who are prodding the field to do so. As noted earlier, public administration is advantaged by the permeability of its disciplinary boundaries evidenced by its willingness to accept into its discipline, scholars and practitioners schooled in other fields. However, there has been a renewed interest in an ideology of the market following the economics-driven trend towards reinventing and privatizing government functions. This has had a narrowing effect on the public administration vision (Ventriss 1998).

In studying the purpose and functions of public organizations, the theories and process of public policy making, and theories of leadership, among others— public administration scholars share with their social work counterparts a largely practitioner orientation. Criticisms of the field have been leveled by its own scholars who have found it lacking in direction, focused on ever more narrow interests, and marking its boundaries in reaction to politically motivated criticisms of government and bureaucrats. Others in public administration are justly disturbed by the politically (as opposed to substantive) conservative drift and have proposed that public administrationists step away from the field, so to speak, and examine the potential for what Arendt (1959) describes as "a lost treasure of the revolutionary tradition"(Ventriss 1998, 98). Revolution would seem antithetical to public administration, who in Terry's (1995) view, are conservators, not activists. Nevertheless, advocacy is a duty when bureaucratic incompetence and mismanagement inflict harm.

Although references to social welfare research appear in the public administration literature, references to child welfare, in particular, are few. We suspect that there are several reasons for this omission. First, issues that are controversial are anathema to public administration's conservative core, and second, public administration theorists have assigned themselves the role of administrators of the state, setting themselves apart from both business and the private, domestic sphere, the latter being viewed as women's work (Stivers 1993). Because the role of the public administrator is frequently the subject of derision associated in the citizens' minds with intrusions into their private lives much the same as the public perception of the social worker, public administrators have little interest in intruding on another discipline that is also marginalized and characterized as intrusive. For those in public administration who might be persuaded to venture into child welfare, they will find the men and women of social work guarding the gates.

Stivers suggests that the business of administering the state has since ancient times been compared with the pursuits of women, that is, as a higher calling to the secondary nature of women's work which is associated with 'housekeeping'. The work of child welfare may be similarly described—as women's work—dealing with issues of food, clothing, shelter, and nurturing the young, work that historically has been considered by men to be beneath them (Stivers 1993, 33). Public administrators share similarities with social workers in defending their status as a profession and in contending with bureaucrat bashing—in the same way that social workers have been maligned for being the unfeeling agents of bad news and bad acts. The involvement of public administration in restructuring child welfare services necessarily involves the acquiescence of the social work profession to share their knowledge and experience with public administrators, and the willingness of public administrators to share responsibility for a system that they have historically, and conspicuously ignored.

## Government's Role in Re-constructing Child Welfare

The propensity of government policy makers to think in narrow program categories has created many of the inefficiencies that have been blamed on local child welfare agencies. Advocates have an interest in promoting legislation and appropriations for their favored programs, and Congress and local legislatures have, on occasion, obliged. The tendency to partialize as a method of organizing results in exclusivity rather than inclusiveness. The public child welfare system is organized around regulatory structures defined by funding streams. Noted earlier were the unsuccessful attempts by administrations to create an office for families in the Office of Human Development Services (DHHS). It became clear in each instance, that they had little to do. They were in direct competition with categorical programs, for example, child abuse and neglect, adoption, and foster care with separate regulatory requirements and appropriations, and were without a mandate to unite them.

The Children's Bureau further exacerbated the division by creating separate, free-standing child welfare resource centers, each devoted to a categorical program, and each with a growing constituency of advocates who tended to polarize in opposition to one another for program dominance and money. Federal categorical funding streams became the template for states to organize their child welfare services similarly at the local service delivery level.[6] But this is nothing new. Schipper and Dick (1995) note that the desire to specialize and categorize is an ancient one. Herodotus (c.484-425 BC) described the proliferation of specialists in Egypt "as a plan of separation: each physician treats a single disorder and no more; thus the country swarms with medical practitioners." A proliferation of service categories and specialists has partialized clients, bits of them divided among program specialties sharing striking similarities with Herodotus's ailing Egyptians.

Although the notion of a block grant, that is, grouping social service programs under one appropriations mechanism, was viewed skeptically by child welfare advocates (with good reason since they are easy targets for budget cutting) in concept, block grants have much to commend them. In theory, block granted appropriations give the states flexibility in the distribution of funds among the programs encompassed in each block grant, permitting them to distribute funds to the localities based on need, not mandate. However, discretion comes with a price, and in the case of the Social Services Block Grant, appropriations have continued to diminish since its inception, with periodic threats of elimination.

The claim has been made elsewhere in this work that collaboration among service providers (health, mental health, juvenile services, child welfare, law enforcement) is a challenging, even daunting objective, but that in many cases the service recipients of one of these agencies are also clients of others. The overlap in services and service administration is expensive, time consuming (for both workers and clients) and, theoretically, unnecessary. Re-constructing the client as a family requiring a 'family' of services alters the discourse from 'my' to 'our' client. A regional human services authority with a goal of eliminating redundancy and filling service gaps, a method used for some time in the state of Idaho, is perhaps, a practical option.

Family preservation as it was envisioned in the 1970s, a relative newcomer to the child welfare discourse, was described as separate from other child welfare services (child abuse, foster care and adoption). Thus, family preservation programs joined the competition with other categorical child welfare programs for both attention and funding. When the Edna McConnell Clark foundation chose to support the Homebuilder's social learning theory approach above other approaches—there were many more than two (see Maybanks and Bryce 1979; Bryce and Lloyd 1981)—it created another set of power relations parallel with that of the Children's Bureau. Indeed, for a time, the foundation appeared to be more powerful in the family-centered arena than the Children's Bureau by dint of its aggressive funding-marketing strategy.

Money does speak. In the federal grants climate that developed during the formative stages of the family preservation movement, publicly-funded social welfare programs were targeted for budget reductions and public agencies were being encouraged to privatize programs whenever possible. This climate was not conducive for starting new service programs in public child welfare agencies unless the services for such programs could be purchased from the private sector, and even then, new programs had to compete for limited 'prevention' money with foster care and institutional programs.

Reducing the number of foster care and institutional programs is a daunting task for most public agencies, particularly since placement is viewed as fool proof when measured against the risks associated with in-home therapies. However, the Edna McConnell Clark Foundation demonstrated that child welfare agencies are willing to take some risks if the money to do so is guaranteed with a marketing plan and the technical supports that gave some assurances of success. An example of strategic planning on a similar scale at the federal level was the promotion of permanency planning. This is in contrast to the scatter shot approaches to promoting innovations that have been used by the bureau in recent years.

## Conclusion

Although child welfare services in the United States have never enjoyed the serious attention that they deserve by policy makers and the public, the 1970s and 1980s were particularly difficult for the child welfare community. Social services, including the Aid to Families with Dependent Children welfare program, were enduring heavy artillery political attack as economic recession increased competition for scarce program funding and case loads burgeoned with new child abuse and neglect reports following passage of the Child Abuse Protection and Treatment Act (CAPTA 1974). The proliferation of new, cheaper street drugs, and the AIDS epidemic left addicted and infected infants abandoned in hospitals—as well as actual orphans, not just orphans of the living, in need of shelter and families.

Child welfare professionals and advocates, concerned with the number of children in foster homes and institutions, sought solutions through new initiatives and programs that could reduce the numbers of children in care thus stemming foster care drift—that is, the occurrence of lengthy and multiple placements. Family preservation was such a program, its effectiveness having been claimed by small, private organizations that contracted with public agencies to work with very troubled families. It became increasingly clear that the families about which they boasted were not the ones whose problems could defeat the most intrepid caseworker, or who stretched the definition of family beyond rational description. They were not the clients most often identified with drug use who live in congested, impoverished urban areas.

Most of the early programs were founded in less populated mid-western and western states unfamiliar with high volume urban poverty and long histories of racial tensions. Neither were they dependent for basic services on old, intractable nonprofit agencies that had little incentive to alter the procedures that had been in use since their inceptions decades earlier. Although the concept of family preservation was laudable, the method used to promote it—promising prevention of foster care—was flawed. Promoters relied on simplistic claims to gain attention and support for the program.

Workers in the public agency were not trained therapists, nor could training of this nature be expected. Caseloads could not be reduced for just a few workers in an agency without creating dissension, and across the board caseload reductions were not possible without limiting intake, which was neither practical, nor ethical nor wise given the limited diagnostic skills of caseworkers. The potential risk to a child is simply too great a risk for the agency to bear. Worker and union resistance to options for flexible scheduling like the 'extraordinary work week' (Chapter 3), reduced the possibilities for creative solutions to problems of scheduling client visits, and increased the burden on overwhelmed client families by requiring, as evidence of their desire to keep their children, their presence at parenting classes, school meetings, and visits with caseworkers during the hours that marginally employed parents must typically work.

It is clear that re-designing the nation's child welfare system to eliminate some of the problems we have cited cannot be accomplished by child welfare agencies alone. The responsibility for change must be born by the larger community of service providers upon whom the agency's clients must depend for help. The St. Paul Project, described earlier, is an instructive example of the difficulties that can be expected when cooperation and coordination among community services becomes an expectation over an extended period of time. The cry, "Can't we all just get along," cannot overcome individual ambitions and internecine rivalries. Furthermore, agency management fears failure, and the recriminations that failure brings.

Changes of the magnitude suggested here could easily backfire and leave the risk-taking agency managers and administrators alone, friendless, and possibly out of work. Such changes also require altering procedures, many of which are required by the state agency that is required to oversee the legitimacy of the local public agency. Without the approval of state officials, many who share the concerns of their local management counterparts, sweeping program changes cannot be made.

For these reasons, and others discussed in previous chapters, strong, national inter-disciplinary leadership and a shared interdisciplinary responsibility for re-imagining and reconstructing the U.S. child welfare system is the only answer. It is time to replace the inadequacies of the child welfare discourse with a family-centered discourse. For too long, child welfare has been the tiresome misfit in social work, women's work in public administration, and too daunting a challenge for family therapy. An orphaned child welfare system has been the unhappy result.

---

## Notes

[1] References the Allegory of the Cave, Plato's Republic, Book VII where the escape from the darkness of the cave into sunlight represents the progress of the soul from the prison of the senses to the world of true enlightenment (357).

[2] Although a few states have recently addressed this problem ( i.e. CO, CT, ID, ME, ND, OR, RI, VT, IA, MN, PA, WI), states have required that families voluntarily relinquish custody of their emotionally, behaviorally, or mentally disabled child in order to obtain long-term treatment services. However, in doing so, the parent looses any authority to control or influence that treatment.

³ The Florida legislature approved a bill to transfer the responsibility for all child abuse investigations from the Department for Child and Family Services to the sheriff's offices in Pinellas, Pasco and Manatee counties as a pilot program to test the feasibility of transferring all investigations from the department to the sheriff's offices in the remaining counties (1998 session, Florida State Legislature).

⁴ Jane Addams (1860-1935), Mary Richmond (1861-1928), and Edith Abbott (1876-1957).

⁵ Children's Bureau grant to Administration for Children, Youth and Families, Pittsburgh, PA, 1989.

⁶ A growing literature in social work on service integration (SI) identifies categorical programs at all levels as an impediment. See O'Looney, John O. (1997). "Marking progress toward services integration: learning to use evaluation to overcome barriers."

# References

Ackerman, N.W., Beatman, F.L., & Sherman, S.N. 1960. *Exploring the case for family therapy.* New York: Family Service Association of America.

Adams, P. 1994. Marketing social change: The case of family preservation. *Children & Youth Services Review* 16(5/6):417-431.

Bassi, V.M. 1991. *The genesis of family therapy: An oral history of the years 1945-1960.* Berkeley: California School of Professional Psychology at Berkley/Alameda. Dissertation.

Berliner, L. 1993. Is family preservation in the best interest of children? *Journal of Interpersonal Violence* 8(4):556.

Bernstein, N. 1998. Guiliani's Foster Care Plan Faces a Political Minefield. *The New York Times* 7 June, 26 (N).

————. A girl's death underscores complexity of child welfare: Agency faces universe of family problems. *New York Times* 21 February, 31 (N).

Billingsley, A. & Giovannoni, J.M. 1972. *Children of the storm: Black children and American child welfare.* New York: Harcourt, Brace Jovanovich.

Bowen, O., and the Department of Health and Human Services 1983. Draft statement by Secretary Bowen for Release at OHDS/DHHS. 5 January.

Bradbury, D.E. 1956. *Four decades of action for children: A short history of the Children's Bureau.* Washington, DC: US Government Printing Office.

Browning, G. 1948. Public administration and human welfare. *The Social Service Review.* (March):10-19.

Bryce, M., & Lloyd, J.C., eds. 1981. *Treating families in the home: An alternative to placement.* Springfield, IL: Charles C. Thomas.

Buell, B., & Associates 1952. *Community planning for human services.* New York: Columbia University Press.

Burlingame, V.S. 1982. *The family therapy tapestry: A multidisciplinary history of the family therapy movement in the United States from 1900 to 1957.* Evanston, IL: Northwestern University. Dissertation.

Burt, M.R. 1976. *A comprehensive emergency services system for neglected and abused children.* New York: Vantage Press.

Cartwright, N. 1996. *Otto Neurath: Philosophy between science and politics.* New York: Cambridge University Press.

Chandler, S.M. 1990. *Competing realities: The contested terrain of mental health advocacy.* New York: Praeger.

Child Welfare League of America. 1981. *Statement on child advocacy.* M. Phillips, editorial consultant. New York: Child Welfare League of America. Committee on Government Operations, 99th Congress. 7 May. News Release.

Compton, B. 1979. A participant observer's brief summary of the family centered project. Unpublished paper.

Cottrell, L.S., Jr. 1967. forward to *Evaluative research: Principles and practice in public service & social action programs*, by Edward A. Suchman. New York: Russell Sage Foundation. p.vii.

Diamond, M.A. 1993. *The unconscious life of organizations: Interpreting organizational identity.* Westport, CT: Quorum Books.

Donzelot, J. 1979. *The policing of families.* New York: Random House.

Dunn, W.N. 1988. *An introduction to public policy analysis.* New York: Prentice-Hall.

Ehrenreich, J.H. 1985. *The altruistic imagination: A history of social work and social policy in the United States.* Ithaca, NY: Cornell University Press.

Emlen, A. 1978. *Overcoming barriers to planning for children in foster care.* Washington, DC: US Government Printing Office.

Epstein, W.M. 1997. Social science, child welfare, and family preservation: A failure of rationality in public policy. *Children and Youth Services Review* 19(1/2):41-60.

Fahl, M.A. & Morrissey, D. 1979. The Mendota model: Home-community treatment. *Home-based services for children and families: Policy, practice, and research.* S. Maybanks & M. Bryce eds. 225-236. Springfield, IL: Charles C. Thomas.

Fanshel, D. 1978. *Children in foster care: A longitudinal investigation.* New York: Columbia University Press.

Farmer, D.J. 1995. *The language of public administration: Bureaucracy, modernity, and postmodernity.* Tuscaloosa, AL: University of Alabama Press.

_____. 1999. The discourse movement: A centrist view of the sea change. *International Review of Public Administration* 4(1): 3-10.

_____. (2000). The ladder of organization think: Beyond flatland. *Administrative Theory and Praxis* 21(1):170-174.

Foucault, M. ed. 1975. *I, Pierre Riviere, having slaughtered my mother, my sister, and my brother...* New York: Pantheon Books.

Fraser, M. 1991. Assessing the effectiveness of family preservation programs: Implications for agency-based research. *Family preservation: Papers from the Institute for Social Work Educators 1990.* A.L. Sallee & J.C. Lloyd eds. Riverdale, IL: National Association for Family-Based Services.

Friedman, R.S. 1993. Homebuilders, family systems and false dichotomies: Reflections on cross-currents in family preservation thinking and steps toward integration. *The Prevention Report.* Iowa City, IA: The National Resource Center on Family Based Services. (Spring):7-8.

Geiser, R.L. 1973. The illusion of caring: Children in foster care. Massachusetts: Beacon.

Geismar, L.L. 1971. *Family and community functioning: A manual of measurement for social work practice and policy.* Metuchen, NJ: The Scarecrow Press, Inc.

Gelles, R.J. 1993. Family reunification/family preservation: are children really being protected? *Journal of Interpersonal Violence* 8(4): 557.

Giovannoni, J.M., telephone interview by author. 9 July 2000.

Glass, C.R. & Arnkoff, D.B. 1995. Behavior therapy. *History of psychotherapy: A century of change.* Donald K. Freedheim, ed. Washington, DC: American Psychological Association: 587-628.

Goding, G. 1992. *The history and principles of family therapy.* Melbourne: A Victorian Association of Family Therapists Publication.

Gramsci, A. 1971. *Selections from the prison notebooks.* Q. Hoare & G.N. Smith, eds. & translators. New York: International Publishers.

Guerin, P.J., Jr. & Chabot, D.R. 1992. Development of family systems theory. *History of psychotherapy: A century of change.* Donald K. Freedheim ed. Washington, DC: American Psychological Association.

Hall, P.D. 1992. *Inventing the non-profit sector.* Baltimore, MD: Johns Hopkins University Press.

Hancock, B.L. & Pelton, L. 1989. Home visits: history and functions. *Social Casework* 70(1):21-27.

Hardy, D. 1983. An internal memo sent to HDS senior staff referring to the "President's Private Sector Survey on Cost Control." 6 April.

————. 1983. An internal DHHS memo referring to the "President's Private Sector Survey on Cost Control." 6 May: p. 80.

Harman, M.M. & Mayer, R.T. 1986. *Organization theory for public administration.* Glenview, IL: Scott, Foresman and Company.

Hartman, A. & Laird, J. 1983. *Family-centered social work practice.* New York: The Free Press.

Holden, C. 1984. Reagan versus the social sciences. *Science.* 226(4678):1052-1054.

Howard, J.A. & Hollander, J. 1997. *Gendered situations, gendered selves: A gender lens on social psychology.* Thousand Oaks, CA: Sage Publications, Inc.

Howe, D. 1994. Modernism, postmodernism, and social work. *British Journal of Social Work* 24:513-532.

Hutchinson, J.R. 1995. A multimethod analysis of knowledge use in social policy: research use in decisions affecting the welfare of children. *Science Communication* 17(1):90-106.

Jeter, H.R. 1963. *Children, problems, and services in child welfare programs.* Washington, DC: Children's Bureau, US/DHEW.

Jones, M.A., Neuman, R. & Shyne, A.W. 1976. *A second chance for families: Evaluation of a program to reduce foster care.* New York: Child Welfare League of America.

Jones, M.A. 1976. Reducing foster care through services to families. *Children Today* 5(6):6-10.

Kamerman, S.B. & Kahn, A.J. 1989. Social services for children, youth and families in the U.S. (unpublished Executive Summary funded by The Annie E. Casey Foundation. Washington, DC).

Katz, M.B. 1996. *In the shadow of the poor house: A social history of welfare in America,* 2nd Ed. New York: Basic Books.

Kellam, S. 1986. Senate postpones hearings on Hardy nomination. *Federal Times* 12 May 1986:3.

Kempe, C.H. & Helfer, R.E. 1972. *Helping the battered child and his family.* Philadelphia: Lippincott.

Knitzer, J. & Allen, M. 1978. Children without homes. Washington, DC: Children's Defense Fund.

La Barre, W. 1960. Biosocial unity of the family. *Exploring the base of family therapy: Papers from the M.Robert Gomberg Memorial Conference.* N.W. Ackerman, F.L. Beatman & S.N. Sherman eds. New York: Family Service Association of America, 8-9.

Larner, G. 1994. Para-modern family therapy: Deconstructing post-modernism, *A.N.Z.J. Family Therapy* 15(1):11-16.

Lemann, N. 1997. Citizen 501(c)(3): An increasingly powerful agent in American life is also the least noticed. *The Atlantic Monthly* (February): 2(297) 18.

Leonard, P. 1994. Knowledge/power and postmodernism: Implications of the practice of a critical social work education. *Canadian Social Work Review* 11(1):11-26.

———. 1995. Postmodernism, socialism and social welfare. *Journal of Progressive Human Services* 6(12): 3-19.

Littner, N. 1956. Some traumatic effects of separation and placement. New York: Child Welfare League of America.

Littell, J.H. & Schuerman, J.R. 1995. A synthesis of research on family preservation and family reunification programs. Online. Internet. 30 January 2000 http://aspe.os.dhhs.gov/hsp/cyp/fplitrev.htm.

Lourie, N.V. 1972. The question of advocacy: The many forces of advocacy. *Public Welfare* 30(2):12-15.

Lubove, R. 1965. *The professional altruist: The emergence of social work as a career 1880-1930.* Cambridge, MA: Harvard University Press.

Luckoff, I.F. & Mencher, S. 1962. A critique of the conceptual foundation of community research associates. *Social Service Review* 36(4):433-457.

Maas, H. & Engler, R. 1959. Children in need of parents. New York: Columbia University Press.

Mangold, G.B. 1934. Organization for social welfare, with special reference to social work. New York: Macmillan.

Mannes, M. 1993. Family preservation: A professional reform movement. *Journal of Sociology and Social Welfare* 22(3):5-24.

Maybanks, S. & Bryce, M. eds. 1979. Home-based services for children and families: Policy, practice and research. Springfield, IL: Charles C. Thomas.

Minkoff, D.C. 1994. From service provision to institutional advocacy: The shifting legitimacy of organizational forms. *Social Forces* 72(4):943-970.

Minuchin, P., Colapinto, J., & Minuchin, S. 1998 *Working with Families of the Poor.* New York: Guilford Press.

Minuchin, Salvador. interview by author. 7 October 1999. Boston, MA.

————. & Elizur, J. 1990. The foster care crisis. *The Networker* (Jan/Feb): 44-62.

————. Montalvo, B., Guerney, B.G., Jr., Rosman, B.L., Schumer, F. 1967. *Families in the slums: An exploration of their structure and treatment.* New York: Basic Books, Inc.

Morgan, G. 1986. *Social policy in the United States: Future possibilities in historical perspectives.* Princeton, NJ: Princeton University Press.

Mott, P.E. & Lunsford, B. 1979. *Home based services for children and their families.* (DHHS, Children's Bureau Contract #105-76-1130, unpublished). The child welfare resource information exchange, Washington, DC.

National Association of Social Workers, NASW Internet Web site. Online. 18 January 1999. http://www.naswdc.org/

Nelson, K.E. & Landsman, M.J. 1992. *Alternative models of family preservation: Family-based services in context.* Springfield, IL: Charles C. Thomas.

New England Association of Child Welfare Commissioners and Directors 1988. A common ground for children and families. *The Newspaper of the New England Association of Child Welfare Commissioners and Directors* 4(3):1.

Nicholson, D. 2000. He's just one child in limbo, but he's the one I know. *The Washington Post* 27 August: B-2.

Notkin, S. (Director of Children's Programs, Edna McConnell Clark Foundation). interview by author. November 2, 1999, New York.

O'Connor, S. 2001. When children relied on faith-based agencies. *The New York Times* 26 May: A23.

O'Looney, J. 1997. Marking progress toward services integration: Learning to use evaluation to overcome barriers. *Administration in Social Work* 21(3/4):31-65.

Overton, A. & Tiner, K. H. 1970. *Casework Notebook.* St. Paul, MN: Greater St. Paul Community Chest and Councils, Inc.

Patterson, G.R. 1972. *Multiple evaluations of a parent training program.* Paper presented at the International Symposium on Behavior Modification, Minneapolis, MN. October 1972.

Paul, J.L., Neufeld, G.R. & Pelosi, J.W. eds. 1977. *Child advocacy within the system.* Syracuse, NY: Syracuse University Press.

————. 1977. Advocacy and the advocate. *Child advocacy within the system.* J.L. Paul, G.R. Newfeld & J.W. Pelosi eds. Syracuse, NY: Syracuse University Press.

Pecora, P.J., Fraser, M.W., Haapala, D., & Bartolme, J.A. 1987. Defining family preservation services: Three intensive home based treatment programs. Research Report Number 1. Washington, DC: Office of Human Development Services, Administration for Children, Youth and Families, DHHS.

Pelton, L.H. 1990. Resolving the crisis in child welfare. *Public Welfare* 48(4):19-25.

Persico, T. 1979. Who knows? Who cares? Forgotten children in foster care. Washington, DC: National Commission on Children in Need of Parents.

Plato. Plato's Apology, in *Dialogues of Plato.* Translated by Jowett and edited by J.D.Kaplan. New York: The Pocket Library. 1959.

Polsky, A.J. 1991. *The rise of the therapeutic state.* Princeton, NJ: Princeton University Press.

Rodgers, R. & Rodgers, N. 2000. Defining the boundaries of public administration: Undisciplined mongrels versus disciplined purists. *Public Administration Review* 60(5):435-445.

Rossi, P.H. 1992a. Assessing family preservation programs. *Children and Youth Services Review* 14:77-97.

———— 1992b. Strategies for evaluation. *Children and youth services review* 14:167-191.

Santoro, W.A. & McGuire, G.M. 1997. Social movement insiders: The impact of institutional activists on affirmative action and comparable worth policies. *Social Problems* 44(4):503-522.

Sartre, J. 1960. *Critique of dialectical reason.* London, UK: NLB.

Schacter, H.L. 1989. Frederick Taylor and the public administration community: a reevaluation. Albany: State University of New York Press.

Scherz, F.H. 1953. What is family-centered casework? *Social Casework* 34(8):343-349.

Schipper, H. & Dick, J. 1995. Herodotus and the multidisciplinary clinic. *The Lancet* 346(8986):1312-1314.

Schorr, A.L. 2000. The bleak prospect for public child welfare. *Social Service Review* 74(1):124.

Sherman, S.N. 1960. The concept of the family in casework theory. *Exploring the base of family therapy: Papers from the M. Robert Gomberg*

*Memorial Conference.* N.W. Ackerman, F.L. Beatman & S.N. Sherman eds. New York: Family Service Association of America.

Shyne, A.W. & Schroeder, A.G. 1980. *National study of social services to children and their families.* Rockville, MD: Westat, Inc.

Silver, I. 1997. Constructing 'social change' through philanthropy: Boundary framing and the articulation of vocabularies of motives for social movement participation. *Sociological Inquiry* 67(4):488-503.

Simmons, H.E. 1961. Social work and administration. *Public Administration Review* 1(Winter):40-44.

Siporin, M. 1980. Marriage and family therapy in social work. *Social Casework: The Journal of Contemporary Social Work* 6(1):11-21.

Skinner, B. F. 1953. *Science and Human Behavior.* New York: Macmillan.

Skocpol, T. 1995. *Social policy in the United States: Future possibilities in historical perspectives.* Princeton, NJ: Princeton University Press.

Steiner, G.U. 1976. *The children's cause.* Washington, DC: The Brookings Institution.

Stivers, C. 1993. *Gender Images in public administration: Legitimacy and the administrative state.* Newbury Park, CA: Sage Publications. p.29-33.

Street, E. 1931. *Social work administration.* New York: Harper & Bros.

Suchman, E. A. 1976. *Evaluative research: Principles and practice in public service & social action programs.* New York: Russell Sage Foundation.

Sudia, Cecelia E. Placement prevention programs in the U.S. 17 December 1985, Internal memorandum.

Taylor, F.W. 1947. *Shop management.* Westport, CN: Greenwood Press Publishers.

Terry, L.D. 1995. *Leadership of public bureaucracies: The administrator as conservator.* Thousand Oaks, CA: Sage Publications, Inc.

Thomas, S.R. 1994. Orphans of public policy. *Policy Currents,* 4(2):1-4.

Tillich, P. 1961. The philosophy of social work. *Social Service Review* 36(1):13-16.

U.S. Dept. of Health and Human Services, Children's Bureau.1994. *National study of protective, preventive and reunification services delivered to children and their families.* Washington, DC: U.S. Government Printing Office.

U.S. Department of Health and Human Services, Children's Bureau. 1997. *National study of protective, preventive and reunification services delivered to children and their families.* Washington, DC: U.S. Government Printing Office.

U.S. Department of Health and Human Services 1983. Task force report on the Department of Health and Human Services Department of Management, Office of Human Development Services and Action. *The President's Private Sector Survey on Cost Control.* Washington, DC: U.S. Government Printing Office. 15 April.

U.S. Department of Health and Human Services 2001. HHS reports new child abuse and neglect statistics. Online. Internet. 2 April 2001 http://www.os.dhhs.gov/news/press/2001pres/20010402.html.

U.S. House. 1986. Intergovernmental Relations and Human Resources Subcommittee. "House panel to reviews management of human development services grants." Press Release. Washington, D. C., US Government Printing Office. 7 May.

U.S. House. 1987. Committee on Government Operations. "Mismanagement of the office of human development services: Undermining programs for children, the disabled, and the elderly." 6th Report. Washington, D. C., US Government Printing Office: 15 April.

Van de Vall, M. & Bolas, C. 1982. Using social policy research for reducing social problems: An empirical analysis of structure and functions. *The Journal of Applied Behavioral Science* 18(1):49-67.

Ventriss, C. 1998. Swimming against the tide: Reflection on some recent theoretical approaches of public administration theory. *Administrative Theory & Praxis* 20(1):91-101.

Wald, M.S. 1988. Family preservation: Are we moving too fast? *Public Welfare* Summer: 33-46.

Waldo, D. 1968 Scope of the theory of public administration. *Theory and Practice of Public Administration.* J.C. Charlesworth (ed). Philadelphia: American Academy of Political and Social Science: 1-26.

Wattenberg, E. & Pearson, Y. 1997. Rethinking child welfare: Can the system be transformed through community partnerships? *A Summary of the Proceedings of a Symposium.* Minneapolis: Center for Advanced Studies in Child Welfare, School of Social Work and Center for Urban and Regional Affairs, University of Minnesota.

Weber, M. 1958. *The Protestant ethic and the spirit of capitalism.* Translated by T. Parsons. New York: Charles Scribner's Sons.

Weiss, C. 1980. *Social science research and decision-making.* New York: Columbia University Press.

Wells, K. & Freer, R. 1994. Reading between the lines: The case for qualitative research in intensive family preservation services. *Children and Youth Services Review* 16(5/6):399-415.

Whittaker, J. K. 1990. The leadership challenge in family based practice: Implications for policy, practice, research, and education. *Family Preservation: Papers from the Institute for Social Work Educators 1990.* A.L.Sallee and J.C. Lloyd eds. Riverdale, IL: National Association for Family-Based Services, 1-16.

Wilensky, H.L. and Lebeaux, C.N. 1958. *Industrial society and social welfare: The impact of industrialization on the supply and organization of social welfare services in the US.* New York: Russell Sage Foundation.

Willard, D.W. 1924. Inter-state reports from the fields of public welfare and social work. *The Journal of Social Forces* 2(5):682-688.

Wholey, J.S., Hatry, H.P., & K.E. Newcomer. (1994). Meeting the need for practical evaluation approaches: An introduction. *Handbook of practical Program Evaluation*, J.S. Wholey, H.P. Hatry & K.E. Newcomer eds. San Francisco: Jossey-Bass, Inc.

Young, I.M. 1994. Gender as seriality: Thinking about women as a
    social collective. *Signs*. 19(3):713-738.
Yuan, Y.T. 1990. Evaluation of AB 1562 in-home care demonstration projects,
    volume 1: Final report. (This report was prepared pursuant to the
    Department of Social Services, Office of Child Abuse Prevention
    Grant No. KED 6012.)

# Author Index

# Index